Berlin to Bradford

Berlin to Bradford

by

Rudi Leavor

For Sharon, Rob, Isabella, Luca and Leo
from Rudi Leavor
January 2021

WORDS by DESIGN

Produced in association with

The right of Rudi Leavor to be identified as the
Author of this Work has been asserted by him in accordance
with the Copyright, Designs and Patents Act 1988.

Typeset in Garamond

Printed and bound in the UK
ISBN: 978-1-914002-02-1

Rudi and Richard Stroud No. 10 Downing Street, London.
Richard is the great-grandson of the first Rabbi of the Synagogue and
has successfully nominated me for several awards. 14 June 2018.

Dedicated to my four children, five spouses, eight grandchildren with their partners where appropriate, two great-grandchildren, sister, nieces and their partners and the memory of Marianne, my parents and Marianne's parents.

CONTENTS

FOREWORD

I t's an honour to contribute a foreword to this memoir. This is an account of a life well and truly lived; a life dedicated to the service of others and to the bringing of understanding, peace and wellbeing between peoples. Rudi Leavor is a remarkable individual. In the following pages you will follow his remarkable journey, growing up as a Jewish child in Germany as the Nazis came to power, his family's flight to the UK and 'accidental' arrival in Bradford, his many years of service to the communities of Bradford and wider service to the Jewish community in the UK and beyond. At a time when our world seems ever more polarised and seismic tremors threaten to fracture relationships between communities Rudi's story remains as contemporary and important as ever. It is a privilege as Chief Executive of Bradford Council that I've been able to play a small part in bringing this project to fruition.

Kersten England CBE
Chief Executive
City of Bradford Metropolitan District Council
Office of the Chief Executive

PREFACE

Though I can trace my great-grandparents on both sides to 1832 the earliest written history of any kind is a review in the local newspaper 'Der Israelit' of my father's bar mitzva dated 19 November 1903 in Inowrazlaw in Poland, unearthed by the curator of the Jewish Museum in Berlin, Germany, Aubrey Pomerance. High praise is given not only to my father but to his father who was President of the community. He had a Sefer Torah (the Five Books of Moses on a parchment scroll) specially written for the occasion. We were able to bring this Sefer with us on our emigration and it is now in the Jewish Museum in Berlin. See Addendum 1.

Many thanks are due to Rosemary O'Dea for tirelessly editing and re-editing the book; to Ruth Vining for recommending me to write it all down for you to read and hopefully enjoy and to my granddaughter Rebecca for designing the frontispiece. Special thanks are due to Bradford Metropolitan Council who subsidised the publication of this book. Many thanks to Tony Gray of WORDS BY DESIGN for patiently helping me to find my way through the publishing process.

My friend Deputy Lieutenant Zulfi Karim, President of the Bradford Council of Mosques, was going to be involved in these memoirs. He is also Chairman of the Muslim Bereavement Services. Though suffering from ongoing

Covid effects he is involved in all burials which are currently well into double figures daily, supervising personally 14 hours per day, light or dark. We wish him a full recovery and an ease of his colossal burden.

INTRODUCTION

My grandson David asked me how we came to England. I told him that it was all contained in my memoirs. He asked how I came to write this book when I told him. He said that that should be part of the story. So here it is:

Having acquired a beautiful timeshare villa in Tenerife in 1985, overlooking the sea and giant rocks called Los Gigantes which became the name of the village, we inevitably got to know many of the other timeshare owners who by definition all came at the same time every year. One such was a lady called Ruth Vining who lived in Cardiff and had worked for the BBC in the publications department. Going round to her villa one day in 2018, over some refreshment she asked me out of the blue to tell her something about my heritage. When half an hour later I had finished telling her my life history which, though I say it myself, was not devoid of interest, and after a pregnant pause she said: 'I hope you have written all this down.' I replied that I hadn't. She said: 'go home and do it!' So when I got home I did it and here it is. Thank you, Ruth.

BEGINNINGS AND FAMILY BACKGROUND

Charles Dickens begins each chapter of his book 'David Copperfield' with a short superscription. Chapter one is headed 'I am born'. I could do worse than introducing my book by emulating him 'I was born' on 31 May 1926 in Berlin, Germany and have immortalised the date in my mobile telephone number's last 6 digits as 503131. The first thing I happen to be able to remember was visiting my maternal grandmother called in the family 'Omuli', but her name was Erwine, lying on her deathbed, but still alive, in Frankfurt am Main, Germany in 1929. She died of stomach cancer shortly afterwards. The next thing I can remember was wishing for a toy tram painted yellow and red for my fourth birthday, which I duly got. The other present was my sister Lore Erwine who was born the day after. It is said that my mother, Luise, did not have time to go to the clinic owned by a Dr. Max Hirsch to be delivered because she was busy with looking after my birthday party. I adored Winnie or Winchen which did not prevent me in later years from teasing her as tends to be usual amongst siblings, probably arranged by nature to prevent incest. Today we are very close emotionally though 200 miles apart for the last 67 years. When I was one-year old great-grandfather Louis Marcus, my grandmother's father, was still alive and is reported to have said: 'Ich habe ihn wenigsten noch kriechen gesehen' (I have at least still seen

1

him crawling). He died shortly afterwards.

Sister Winnie went to school only for a short time in Berlin – she was only seven when we emigrated. Going to school in Shipley [later part of Bradford] the headmaster Wilfred B. Tapp was kindness personified and she soon became word perfect (for her age). Tapp was an amateur artist and later we acquired some of his paintings. When he retired, he lived in a house in Kettlewell in Wharfedale where we visited him. But one winter when he needed medical help the doctor, could not get through the snow-blocked roads and Tapp had to relocate to his daughter's house in Bingley. Winnie went to the Bradford Girls' Grammar School. At that time we were friends with the Flehinger family. Most tragically Anne Flehinger was killed in a car accident. My mother visited the widowed Arthur and occasionally took Winnie with her. They had two sons: Gerald and Walter. Soon Winnie and Gerald became attracted to one another and became engaged, but Gerald was studying French in Paris, France and Winnie was about to begin studying physiotherapy at the Middlesex Hospital in London. My parents bought a house in Golders Green for Winnie to use and she fortunately was able to take in two lodgers: Walter and myself. I was studying a postgraduate course for six months at the (dental) Eastman Clinic.

Winnie and Gerald eventually married in 1953 and had two girls: Diana and Jacqueline. Diana lived in Israel for a year, then came back, became a teacher and eventually deputy head. She married Claude whose parents immigrated from Italy many years previously and they have two daughters: Luisa and Jessica. Luisa married her girlfriend Yael in 2018. Jacqueline studied Art, is an artist and lives in Otley, Yorkshire, with her partner Kenny who is a lecturer in Music.

My parents sent me to a Montessori Kindergarten where, so far as I can remember, I was quite happy until another child struck me on the lip with a toy brick which made it bleed. My mother complained but was told that the ethics in the nursery was that children could do what they wanted, so I was unceremoniously removed from there. I see that at least one such nursery still exists locally and UK wide probably more.

My mother was born in Munich, Germany, on 23 August 1901, two years after her elder sister Henny who had a slightly deformed hip which hindered her walking somewhat but did not prevent her later from studying chemistry and obtaining a degree, something girls would not normally do at that time and age. Nor did it prevent her from marrying Dr. Leo Winter, son of Dr. Jacob Winter the Chief Rabbi of Dresden, Germany, who, when there was that change of Government in 1933, was made to scrub the pavement outside his synagogue to the obvious amusement of bystanders. The family decided there and then to emigrate to Palestine. Henny also played the piano very well, going through the Schumann piano concerto's solo part flawlessly. They had one child, Gabriele who married Fritz Bauer who came from Vienna, Austria. They had two children Gad and Ruth. Both are married with children.

When Luise was aged two the family moved to Frankfurt am Main where their father Josef, called 'Opeps', was a highly respected member of the Jewish community, being very orthodox which his wife Erwine was not. My mother worked on a voluntary basis for a forward-looking social worker Bertha Pappenheim, in Isenburg, a suburb of Frankfurt. Part of her functions was to collect babies from unmarried mothers who would give their baby up for adoption. She relates that often when she would carry a baby on the train from where it was born to Isenburg, without a wedding ring, other passengers would look at her askance.

My father, Hans, was born in Inowrazlaw, sometimes called Hohensalza, in the Polish Corridor, a strip of land belonging some of the time to Russia or Germany, depending on who won the last war, on 30 October 1890. His father, Rudolf, after whom I am called, was also very orthodox and was the *mohel* (circumcisor) for the large Jewish community. He died aged 53 from kidney failure which distressed my father greatly. Rudolf's wife, Bertha, was not particularly orthodox. Bertha lived with three of her sisters and came to our flat every Erew Shabbat (Friday evening, the beginning of the Sabbath) bringing me two miniature *challahs* (plaited bread traditionally eaten on Shabbat and Festivals.) My father had three younger sisters: Hedwig (Hede), Margarete (Grete) and Elli. Hede married Gustav Stein, a dental surgeon but they had no children; eventually they emigrated to Palestine. Grete did not marry and complained to me many years later that all the money in the family went towards my father's studies in medicine; so much so that none was left for a dowry for her. I don't know how true this was. Elli married a non-Jewish orthopaedic surgeon Alfred Stimming in Berlin, Germany. They had two children born in the same year 1931: Helga and Wolfgang. During the war they hid in Alfred's parents' house in Detz about 70 km. from Berlin. The children missed out on their schooling for a couple of years. Helga who never married became a physiotherapist and died of breast cancer aged in her 70s and Wolfgang also became an orthopaedic doctor. He married Erika with whom he had three children: Janine, Peter and Jacqueline. All are married and in live in Germany. They divorced and Wolfgang married Marlis. Elli and Alfred died of cancer within six weeks of each other. Wolfgang died in 2018.

My father studied in Munich qualifying as a doctor and was promptly enlisted into the army for the Great War 1914-1918 during which he was awarded the Iron Cross second class for some act of bravery which he never discussed and about which we never asked him. After the war he studied dentistry and settled in Berlin.

My parents met in the spa town Baden-Baden, Germany. My mother and her mother were sitting on a promenade bench minding their own business when my father strolled along, also minding his own business, when he spotted my mother and liked the look of her. After a few metres he turned round, retraced his steps and walked past again taking a closer look. After a few more metres he turned round again and this time plucked up courage to speak to them. He managed to arrange a later meeting. Her mother chided her implying that she flirted with him at that first encounter. Although my father was the more intellectual in the marriage my mother was the more dominant and it worked thus very well.

Schooling in Berlin

In due course aged six I was enrolled in the local primary school. There were four Jewish boys in my class and I was quite friendly with two of them: Felix Frankfurter and Wolfgang Bloch. The fourth one left after one year – Michael Baumann. I sat next to a boy called Goetz who was a bit unruly. I complained to the class teacher, a Fräulein Rage (pronounced as two syllables, not the English way). She suggested that I enter into my daybook any misdemeanour he perpetrated. Sure enough, the next day he plonked an inkblot into my book – I was furious. I wrote a note next to it – Goetz macht Kleckse ins Heft (Goetz puts [ink-] blotches into the book). Unfortunately, I omitted the 'l' so that it read Keckse which means biscuits, even then misspelt.

Marianne and I had been married a year or so when she got a message from the chairman of the group B'nai B'rith, Freddie Haas, through which we had met in London, that another couple, Hedy and Felix Franks who had also been members of the group, now lived in Huddersfield and probably did not know many people and 'would we invite them over.' We did and spent a pleasant evening together. The next day Felix telephoned to thank us and asked if our name had always been Leavor. Of course, it had not. He said that he had played trains with a Rudi Librowicz in Berlin and was I the same person. I was. Now I did not know that Felix had emigrated to England and 20 years had elapsed. Marianne had obviously not remembered them well enough from meetings of the group. He had also changed his name from Frankfurter. The joy of meeting up again after so many years was great, and we became close friends. His wife Hedy was born in Brno, Czechoslovakia, where her father was a dentist and had been imprisoned in Terezin concentration camp. Felix became a professor Physical Chemistry and a world authority on 'Water' and had written an authoritative book on it. He was also very musical. Sadly, Felix died just after his 90th birthday. Apart from the fact that we did not recognise one another it was peculiar that in spite of spending the whole evening together we did not once explore our heritage, which would have established our previous relationship at once. Sadly, his widow Hedy died in 2018 also aged 90. I attended both their funerals reciting (singing) *el male rachamim*.

One day the teacher told us to bring five Pfennigs to

school. The next day there was a diamond-shaped board on the teacher's desk with fields in red, white and black on it. There were three boxes of nails with heads in the same three colours and each boy could choose which coloured nail he could hammer into the corresponding field. When it came to the Jewish boys' turn the teacher, Herr Albert Butzke, said we three did not have to do this. When all the nails had been hammered in it showed a black swastika on a white background surrounded by a red field. On another occasion I was going to the once weekly Jewish religion class, which was taken in a spare room halfway between two floors where the broad staircase turned through 180 degrees. I tried to open the door but found it locked and realised that I had mistaken the floors. I had gone one higher as they all looked the same. Turning to go down one floor I was met by the deputy head, Herr Sy, coming up with a trail of pupils behind him. He stopped and I had to stop, as I could not pass him or them. There was stalemate whilst we eyed each other. I was very frightened at this turn of events especially as Herr Sy was grotesquely obese with a bald head and fierce moustache. For a moment neither of us spoke then he said, 'Where are you going?' – and I honestly thought he would fortify his words with a gratuitous slap across the face, an action which would have been quite in accordance with the prevailing culture which had nothing to do with antisemitism. In the event he was 'only' very gruff. I said according to the truth that I had lost my way going to the Jewish religion class. I thought the expected slap would come now – I must have been as white as a sheet with fear, but on the contrary his mien changed dramatically and patting my head with kindness personified, said, 'Well then, go to it,' and he let me pass.

One day forms were distributed with spaces for a family

tree with a short sentence on the reverse to say that adolf hitler wishes this to be filled in. Under each entry there was a space to indicate the religion of the person entered. This was quite obviously for the State to establish if there was any Jewish blood in the family. However, my father quite dutifully filled this form in. It had to be handed to the teacher within a few days: it had the most beneficial advantage that a family tree was written going back to great-grandparents which would otherwise probably not have been done. [N.B. I always spell the dictator's name in lower case letters.]

I had a two km walk from home to school. Today there is a bus route along exactly where I used to go. One day when I arrived home my mother asked me to go across the main road, Hohenzollerndamm, to buy half a pound of 'Hackefleisch', (minced meat). Meeting three classmates who had walked a bit slower, we stopped to say hello when one of them, Ulli Meyer, casually asked me where I was going. I told him mentioning the name 'Hackefleisch' when he quite unexpectedly gave me a strong slap across the face saying as he did so, 'Jetzt hast Du Backefleisch' – now you have cheekmeat. He was quick to make Backe rhyme with Hacke. Retaliation was not on my agenda and I went on my way. The slap hurt but more distressing was that a classmate of mine with whom I was in a good but not particularly close relationship should hit me. It was very many years later that I worked out a possible scenario: the media at that time were beginning literally to infect the population with antisemitism which had been lingering under the surface but up to 1933 had not been blatant. Now the newspapers and radio would waste no time but to insert antisemitic items into their pages and programmes. One newspaper 'Der Stürmer' only covered such items disguised as news. It was a vile publication which would be prominently displayed on newsstands. This situation would probably have been discussed at the home of Ulli by his parents and he would have listened in and thought that if an opportunity arose he would go along with the sentiments of the time and also do his bit in haranguing a Jew as exhorted by the media and such an opportunity conveniently came his way that lunchtime. It would be to his eternal shame.

My great love of music was lit at a very early age for whenever I was ill with one children's malaise or other, to prevent my getting bored in bed I was given a musical box which had been, so I found out later, in the family for decades. It was built on the principle of a rotating metal cylinder from which protruded tiny pins which, when the cylinder was revolving, would 'ping' on a series of metal protrusions, each one larger than its neighbour thus giving a pitched musical scale sounding in pitch exactly like a piano's keys. By skilful arrangement of the pins the box could play six tunes each lasting about 1½ minutes. After each song the cylinder would move a fraction to one side in order to activate a different set of pins and thus play another tune. After the sixth song the cylinder would move back to its original position and start again. The sites of thee pins on the cylinder must have been placed in absolutely exact positions for them to play a tune but also not to ping when they were not supposed to ping. The force for the movement was a spring which was wound up like a clock. I have always marvelled at the sheer ingenuity and beauty of this mechanism and of course loved the songs which I have never been able to identify. I still know them by heart.

A similar very complicated system works the so-called Silver Swan in a museum in Barnard Castle in North Yorkshire. This life-size metal swan would, when activated by a motor, dip its head down and pick up a mechanical fish from make-believe water and rear up again. It is a marvel of engineering.

After four years I had to leave and was fortunate to go to a Jewish secondary school, the Grosse Hamburgerstrasse Schule, named after the street in which it was situated. The name was a joke because the street was one of the narrowest imaginable. Here I learnt English which was of course most useful when we emigrated to England. We had a very strict music teacher called Alfred Loewy. Another boy called Günther Unger and I were the best singers in the class and it was always a matter of suspense who of the two of us would be asked to demonstrate how a song should be sung. Loewy was one of the people who influenced my love of music. Tragically I learnt after the war that he was deported to Auschwitz where, though he played the piano very well, which might have earned him a place in the camp orchestra, he was nevertheless murdered. The headmaster was Herr Stern nicknamed 'Bobby'. In due course the school deemed it advantageous to have a non-Jewish head to help it survive. A Herr Feige who was half Jewish was appointed, but this tragically did not prevent him from also being murdered later in the Holocaust. Günther, his parents and younger brother Heinz, later called Ralph (as he did not want to be identified with a well-known food firm) emigrated to New Zealand where his father continued to practice his profession – dentistry. Günther also studied dentistry and a second room was established in the practice for him to move into. Soon after passing his finals a group of twenty or so fellow graduates took a sailing boat out to sea to visit a nearby island and on the return trip a violent storm blew up. The boat, driven on to rocks, was smashed and all the occupants perished. Some years later Ralph and his wife Pat visited the UK and we made acquaintance together with another refugee Ruth Simmonds, née Eger. Her parents and Ralph's parents had been the best of friends in Berlin.

I happened to be walking in the vicinity of the primary school after I had left it and met by chance the class teacher Herr Butzke. We stopped to talk and he naturally enquired how I had got on in my new school. Whilst thus talking a friend of his passed by and, as was obligatory, gave the hitler salute saying the appropriate words to go with it – one always had to do and say this instead of saying 'good morning, etc. Butzke waved his friend on without giving the salute or saying what he should have said in deference to me. He could have been prosecuted for his inaction.

Although I did not sense any antisemitism at the primary school apart from Ulli's untimely aggression which, in any case, took place outside school, I nevertheless felt safe and secure in the Jewish school. The building found itself in the Russian zone of Berlin after the war. Come the 'Wende', the fall of the Iron Curtain in 1989, the building was most fortunately found to be undamaged by the ravages of war. It had been used as some kind of warehouse. The Jewish community was enjoined to re-open it as a secondary school which they proceeded to do forthwith, appointing a non-Jew as the first headmaster – Dr. Uwe Mull. The original piano was still in situ but was in a deplorable state. It was a Steinway, one of the best makes of piano. The firm Steinway was instructed to renovate it which they did free of charge. I was invited to the opening and before any ceremonies had begun I was allowed to play and sing: I performed 'Das Heidenröslein' by Franz Schubert with words by (the Jewish) Heinrich Heine. Understandably it was a very emotional moment. I was invited to a few reunions of past pupils. At one of these it occurred to me that the music room could be called 'Alfred Loewy Zimmer'. The school agreed and searching for a photograph found a composite one in the possession of Henry Gunby, né Heinz Günzburger in New York, USA. He and I had been in the same class and we visited him after my retirement from work. He employed a police lady who would draw a picture of a suspect from a victim's description, which she did to produce a very good likeness of him. A day was appointed to name the room officially. I was invited but could not go. At the last minute a niece of Loewy – Esther Bejarano, who was an Auschwitz survivor living in Hamburg, Germany – got in touch and she was warmly invited to perform at the opening ceremony. I have visited her twice; she is at 95 the Chairperson of the Auschwitz Survivors Association in Germany and still gives singing recitals. She is one of the last survivors of the Women's Orchestra of Auschwitz.

Another teacher was Herr Arnold Amolsky who taught religious studies. He was terribly crippled presumably since birth. As he could not go on public transport, he had to use taxis to come to school. One day I missed my usual city train and was late arriving at school. I raced through the front door and started ascending the staircase when I nearly overtook Amolsky who had great difficulty going up the stairs. If I had overtaken him I would have arrived in the classroom before him and he would not have been able to award me a 'Tadel' (rebuke) for being late. But I could not with a clear conscience do that and instead helped him up the stairs. He was deported to Auschwitz where he would have been one of the first to be murdered because his deformity offended Nazi ideology.

My old school in England, Bradford Grammar, has an annual Speech Day when exceptional pupils can be awarded a prize, funded by old boys of the school or anybody. These are printed in the programme for the day and if desired the prize can be donated in memory of someone. I have donated money to the school (2017/19) enough to award a prize to a promising music student in memory of Loewy and Amolsky in perpetuity. Esther and the German school are aware of this.

In Berlin ours was a reasonably orthodox household keeping a kosher kitchen. We had a maid called Erna Bansemer who came from a small town in Eastern Germany called Schneidemühl, now in Poland called Pula. She was a good soul, did the housework, cooking and washing well. We children loved her. When she had to leave because a new law forbade non-Jewish maids to work in Jewish households for fear of them being violated by the man of the house there were tears all round. I forget what we children gave her as a leaving present, but she gave me a pencil eraser enclosed in what must have been the earliest example of plastic with the name Berlin engraved on it. It was too good to use and many years later, about 2005, I presented it in pristine condition to the new Jewish Museum in Berlin.

The degree of orthodoxy of my maternal grandfather, Josef Schwab, whom we called Opeps was demonstrated vehemently one day. Soon after he was widowed, he decided to emigrate to Palestine where Henny and family had already been for some years. On his journey he spent a few days in our flat. I had been given piano lessons by my parents' best friends, non-Jews called Bandow, whose third son Klaus, who became spokesman for BMW in Munich, only died in 2017 aged 95. I had been taught a piece by Robert Schumann 'Der Fröhliche Landmann' to be played for my mother on her birthday, which happened to fall on a Saturday. After lunch I went to the piano and played this piece as a surprise for her. As soon as I had finished with heaps of praise being showered on me by my parents my grandfather poured cold water on the scene admonishing my mother for allowing me to play the piano on Shabbat. There were arguments flying back and forth which neither side could win. To settle it my grandfather said, 'Ihr könnt machen, was Ihr wollt. Ich halte meinen Sabbat,' (You can do what you want. I keep my Sabbath) and stormed out of the room. But he cooled down and later that day all was forgotten. We shared a love of trains which he put into effect. German railways had invented a new concept of carriage and locomotive combined into what we would today call a diesel train (though it might in fact be powered by electricity). The first one of these was to run between Berlin and Hamburg. He and I went to the Lehrter Bahnhof where, he had ascertained, this new train, called 'Der Fliegende Hamburger', would arrive at a certain time. We got to the platform in good time and presently this modern luxurious looking train slowly and silently came into the station. It looked absolutely unworldly in blue and white, colours not associated with 'ordinary' trains. When all passengers had disembarked we asked for permission to look inside. All seats were upholstered where we had only been used to wooden third-class seats. The floor was carpeted with doormats at the entrance. It was the height of luxury. Very many years later when we holidayed in Dorf Tirol, Italy, we ascertained that the world-famous Simplon Orient Express train, reconstructed after lying fallow for many years, would pass through Bolzano nearby. Jonathan aged about eight and I made our way to the station not even knowing if it would stop there. But luck was on our side. Headed by an enormous (electric) engine it made a pit stop, probably for operational reasons. A passenger came out of the train on to the platform just where we were standing and we inevitably got into conversation with him. He was an American gentleman and we got to asking each other lots of questions about his travel, the train, his destination which was Venice where I had been a few times and loved it. We struck up a close friendship in those few minutes, helped no doubt by liking each other's accents. When he embarked I said, 'Bon voyage and give my love to Venice!' I hope he did.

My paternal grandfather, Rudolf Librowicz, who died of kidney failure in 1913 (so I never knew him) was also very orthodox, a leader of the Jewish community and, as related, was their mohel (the person who would circumcise Jewish boys at the age of eight days). I was told once that it had been established in ancient times that at that age the blood would coagulate the quickest because the count of platelets in the blood that promote coagulation is very high.

My father had his practice in the flat in which we lived in Berlin at Warmbrunnerstrasse 50-52 off the Hohenzollerndamm in Grunewald. He would work on Saturday mornings, but I was sent to synagogue where, with help of religious classes (in addition to those at school) taken partly by Rabbi Dr. Emil Bernard Kohn, I soon learnt to follow the service with ease.

Although Rabbi Kohn's sermons were obviously addressed to the adults such was his choice of words and crystal-clear delivery that even as a child, I could usually follow the argument. A unique experience happened during one service when the chanting from the Torah (the Five Books of Moses hand-written on a long parchment scroll) came to an abrupt stop. The cantor, Herr Casper, and a few men who stood nearby, huddled over the Torah and presently looked around the congregation as if looking for someone as indeed they were. Eventually all their gazes focussed on me and beckoned for me to come up to the bimah (reading desk). In age-old fashion I turned round to see if they perhaps meant someone behind me, but no! it was me they wanted. I duly went up and was shown a particular letter in the Torah and asked what it was. I said it was a 'dallet'. They seemed to agree with me and sent me back to my seat. The Torah was rolled up and exchanged for a different one being fetched from the Ark. After the service they explained to me that the letter should have been a 'he' but the left-hand down stroke had chipped off making it look like a 'dallet' which made the Torah 'posul', i.e. not 100% accurate. I have never come across this since. For Simchat Torah, joy of the Torah, when the end is read, the Torah scrolled back to the beginning and started to be read from the beginning immediately, my grandmother would come to Synagogue with a bag of sweets and when as part of the procession of children following all the Torahs being carried round the Synagogue I passed her she would drop sweets into my basket. I was more overjoyed to see the happy expression on her face than with the confectionary. As she lost her husband early in marriage she doted on my father and me more than normal. She died in Theresienstadt (Terezin) concentration camp, was cremated unceremoniously and her ashes thrown into the local river.

One day in the middle of a service two men in civilian clothes entered the Synagogue, whispered something to the rabbi (presumably they were from the Gestapo – Geheime Staatspolizei – Secret State Police) and took him away. His two daughters saw what was happening and rushed from the ladies' gallery to see him being driven away in their car. All they could think of was to shout after him that he should know that he should not drive (or be driven) in a car on Shabbat. Some months later he re-appeared in the middle of a service and everybody stood up as one. The family emigrated to Los Angeles, USA where, after a few years he was knocked down by a car and killed. The driver was prosecuted but got off on a technicality. Many years later I was briefly in touch with the daughters. Their brother, Bährchen, with whom I was quite friendly attending his bar mitzvah, became a rabbi in New York, but succumbed to a virulent bout of influenza.

Two mild antisemitic incidents come to mind. I was sitting at the hairdressers when another client came in and happened to stand just behind me when he gave the hitler salute which was compulsory instead of 'good morning' etc. In the big mirror it looked as if he gave it with his left hand when the hairdresser remarked that only Jews would give the salute with the left hand. Another time when I went to the Jewish secondary school there were no lessons on Saturdays, but instead there were lessons on Sundays. I went through the ticket barrier for the train with the satchel on my back showing my weekly pass. The ticket man called me back. I knew exactly what would follow and it did. He said, 'Where are you going?' I said, 'To school.' He replied, 'Only Jews go to school on a Sunday'. A more sinister experience was when we went, as we often did, to the open-air swimming establishment at the Wannsee lake in Grunewald. At the ticket office there was a large and unmissable sign which said 'Hunde und Juden unerwünscht' (dogs and Jews unwanted). That Jews were (now) prohibited we expected as a sign of the advancing antisemitic times. What was interesting was the order of nouns – dogs came before Jews. Of course, we returned home. It was this Wannsee where a villa was used in ca. 1941/2 as the venue for a meeting of the higher echelons of the Nazi party to formulate a programme for the total destruction of the Jews. It was the so-called Wannsee Conference. The villa is now a museum commemorating the Holocaust.

The following is the text of a talk I was invited to give after Evensong in Bradford Cathedral on 29 January 2017.

M y Friends, I have several times had the privilege of speaking briefly from this pulpit and emphasise that I have always been received here with warmth and kindness, culminating in being allowed and very honoured and privileged to address you today.

I have chosen a topic which is very personal but for which I make no apology. For 'personal', read 'general' as similar circumstances will have happened to thousands of Jewish people with variations. It is my farewell to Germany. At the same time I want to tell you of two unique experiences which are 78 years apart which happened to me and which I like to compare to Moses from the Old Testament and Saul from the New though both occurrences are as different from each other as can ever be imagined.

We lived in Berlin where my father had a prosperous dental practice. We were fully integrated into German society; my father was a doctor in the First World War on the German side and won the Iron Cross for some act of bravery that he never talked about. One morning in 1936 the doorbell rang at our flat. Erna the maid opened the door and two men (I can't call them gentlemen) said they were from the Gestapo and wanted to see my parents. Erna said they were still in their bedroom. They said, 'Das stört uns nicht' – 'that does not matter to us'. They barged their way in and demanded to know which door led to their bedroom. As I and they met in the corridor, not knowing who they were and being well brought up, I said, 'good morning' and, as was the custom, offered my hand in greeting which they took in turn. They entered the bedroom, told my parents to get dressed and be ready to join them in their car. My father was President of his Lodge and my mother was Treasurer of the corresponding Ladies' Lodge. She was told to bring any monies that she held in trust with her. It amounted to about 30 Marks.

They were taken to the headquarters of the Lodge at Kleiststrasse 10 where other lodge members were already assembled with more to arrive. They were told to stand in rows for several hours. If someone wanted to go to the bathroom, they had to hold up their hand and ask for permission. Sometimes this was granted, sometimes not. My mother was told to hand over the money, for which she had the presence of mind and the courage to ask for a receipt which she put to good use several years later.

After several hours they were told that the Lodge was dissolved and they should go home. This was the scenario which, fortunately, prompted my parents to emigrate. The short arrest was truly a blessing in disguise. If the Gestapo had not arrested my parents, we might not have escaped the fate of millions of Jews in the gas chambers and ovens of Auschwitz.

Fast forward to our actual emigration. On the train my family – younger sister, parents and I – were leaning out of the windows of the second-class compartments as a final treat (instead of third class, our normal way of travelling), taking us to Hamburg. As the train slowly started to move there was a sea of white handkerchieves from friends. This was the traditional way of waving goodbye. We noticed that one family in the group was missing – but they stood at the very end of the platform so that they would be the last ones we would see on leaving. They were the family Radziejewski whom I shall mention again later. This then was the beginning of a roller coaster of emotions lasting 48 hours – escape to freedom but departing from relatives and friends whom we were not likely ever to see again.

We overnighted in Hamburg and next day took the boat train to Bremerhaven. Halfway on this journey a customs officer came into the compartment and after checking our papers asked my father to accompany him to another compartment. Presently the train stopped at a station and when it began to move again and father was not back in our compartment, I said to mother, 'wo ist Vati?' 'where is Father?' She was as anxious as I was but bravely put on an appearance of reassurance, but our minds were in turmoil. The Germans would not have been above restraining him in which case we would have got so far and fallen at the last hurdle. We would have been devastated. However, he came back saying the official had merely examined him more closely in case he had any hidden contraband on his person.

In Bremerhaven we boarded a German cruise liner bound for America but calling at Southampton where we were to disembark. So, we were still on German territory and anything untoward could still happen to us though we had all the right papers and visas.

Now I want to tell you that my father was an excellent pianist and we often played the piano for four hands. Our favourite piece was called 'Dornröschens Brautfahrt', 'Cinderella's Bridal Procession', by Max Rhode. We played this endlessly and we knew it by heart. It became, in modern parlance, 'our tune'.

Wearily, carrying our plentiful luggage, we made our way to the cabin and debilitated by the previous 36 hours of stress, rested a while before slowly making our way to the dining room. Our bodies were as exhausted as our minds. We were shaken to the core with conflicting emotions coursing through our veins – the stress behind us, but still ever-present and potential escape yet to come. Our fragile nerves shattered to shreds as we stumbled along the gangway like zombies. Though it was obviously lit it seemed dark and foreboding not knowing what unpleasant surprise might still be lurking round the next corner. With some trepidation we entered the dining room and as we did the live band struck up our tune: *'Dornröschens Brautfahrt'*. It was an experience as if we had entered Paradise, especially for a family in which music played an important part. We came out of metaphorical thick glutinous darkness into brilliant, warm and welcoming light. Comparisons are odious, as the proverb says, but I can only compare it to how Moses felt on seeing the Burning Bush and his confrontation with God or Saul's conversion on the road to Damascus, both events a cornerstone of our respective religions, such was the change of ambience. The depression flew out of the window like greased lightning, our nerves repaired and our emigration adventure had turned a welcome corner.

To guild the lily the next morning after breakfast my father invited us to the stern of the ship where he dramatically took out of his pocket a bunch of keys which had opened the door to our now vacant flat, and carefully taking one key after another off the keyring he threw them one by one into the sea swearing that he would never set foot in Germany again. And he kept his self-imposed promise.

The family who stood at the end of the platform as we left Berlin met a tragic end. Their son Hans who was a good friend of mine had found himself a job on the large Jewish Weissensee Cemetery to keep out of harm's way, digging graves by day and sleeping rough in one of the many partially hollow graves by night. One day he received a message that Jews were being rounded up including his family – parents, two sisters and a brother. He hurried home and found his family, together with many others, on lorries ready to be driven off. The intention was clear: they were to be driven to a railway station to be transported east to concentrations camps. Exchanging a few words with them but keeping his distance in case the Germans realised that he was one of them, he said before sorrowfully parting, 'lasst mir die Rosemarie hier. Ich kann auf sie aufpassen.' 'leave Rosemarie here. I can look after her.' But the father did not allow it. The lorry drove off and that was the last time he saw them. He himself was eventually also caught and spent some years in Auschwitz which he survived. He discovered later that his family were put on a train consisting of cattle trucks, driven without food, ventilation or sanitation to the outskirts of Riga, Latvia near a forest called Rumbula where those who were still alive detrained to the loud and unwelcoming shout of 'raus, raus' – 'out, out'; they had to stand at the edge of a wide trench in which there were already corpses of previously killed people. They themselves were machine-gunned and conveniently fell into those trenches, increasing thus the count of corpses. This event was one of millions collectively known today, as I am sure you know, as the Holocaust, which is commemorated every year in January on the anniversary of the liberation of Auschwitz in which I take part by singing the Hebrew chant 'el male rachamim'. To date I sing it at Holocaust Memorial Day Events at Bradford, Leeds, Kirklees (Huddersfield), Calderdale (Halifax) and Wakefield. These areas arrange their events so as not to clash in order that I can sing at each of them. [In 2018, I was asked to sing it also in Bradford Cathedral immediately after the event in Leeds].

The other event came last year when I attended a concert by the Dresden Philharmonic Orchestra in Leeds. My mother had a sister who married the son of the late Chief Rabbi of Dresden, Professor Dr. Jakob Winter. Dresden incidentally is well known to Bishop Nick [Baines] (Bishop of Leeds and surrounding area). My aunt had one daughter, my late cousin Gaby. One of the first acts of the Germans in 1933 was to make this revered Rabbi scrub the pavement in front of his synagogue. Some misguided local people, witnessing this objectionable spectacle, joined in showering abuse at the rabbi. The family decided there and then to emigrate to Palestine vowing never to return. Their hatred of Dresden rubbed off on to my family and rightly or wrongly the name of the town became for me a dirty word. However, music got the better of me and I went to this concert. It began with the prologue to Wagner's opera 'Die Meistersinger'. It starts, you may recall, with a loud chord. It was followed by superb playing and without sounding melodramatic, as I listened to this glorious music the curse of Dresden after 85 years was lifted as in a flash of lightning and tears welled up in my eyes at the unexpected startling turn of events. Dresden in my ambience was rehabilitated. Again, in retrospect, Moses' and Saul's experiences came to mind.

My friends: I have adduced biblical events to the present day. Some people have discarded religion but whether they have or not you cannot wish religion and its marvellous history away – it is there. To take an easy example: The Ten Commandments are the basis of everyday life in all civilised communities. Ignore them or it at your peril. Amen.

I am being held by my paternal grandmother, Bertha who is sitting alongside my father and great-grandfather, Louis Marcus in Berlin, 1926

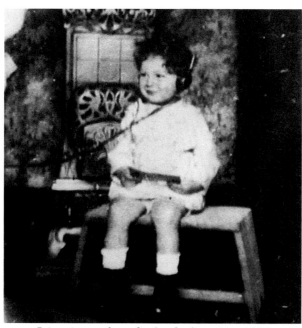

Listening to the radio for the first time, 1929

Great-grandparents Eva and Moritz Librowicz

I am seven years old and Winnie is three years old in Grunewald, Berlin circa 1935

I am seven years old and Winnie is three years old in Grunewald, Berlin c. 1935

25

The family tree form handed out at school stated,
"No boy or girl should
leave school without reveal-
ing his or her heritage
because of the necessity to
investigate the purity of
their blood." Adolf Hitler

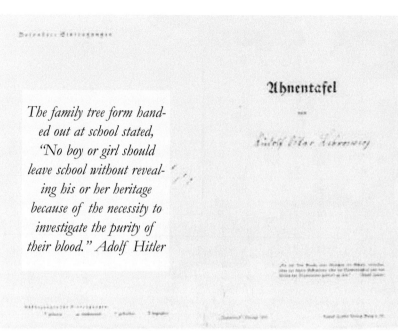

Obverse of family tree

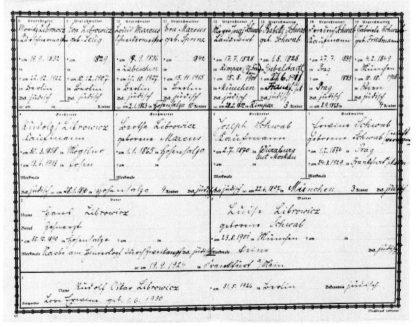

The family tree my father dutifully filled in, circa 1935

26

Meeting Esther Bejarano, the niece of my music teacher, 2017

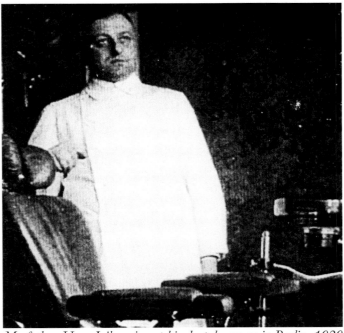

My father, Hans Librowicz at his dental surgery in Berlin, 1929

Back row left to right, Alfred Stimming, Arthur Blumenthal (father of Evi), Elli (wife of Alfred), Else and Hedwig, (daughters of Hannush), Werner Simon (husband of Evi); front row, left to right, Evi (niece of Bertha), Hulda Gembitzky, Hannush (Johanna) Marcus, (both sisters of Bertha – my grandmother), Wolfgang Stimming (son of Alfred and Elli), Bertha Librowicz, Helga (daughter of Alfred and Elli), Henriette (sister of Bertha) circa 1942

Hunde und Juden Unerwünscht. Dogs and Jews not wanted. Sign outside Wannsee outdoor swimming pool 1936 (Rebecca Leavor)

Rudi at the corner of Warmbrunnerstrasse in front of the house where the family lived in Berlin up to 1937

Die Aufstellung dieser Schilder
wurde durch die Spende vom
"Weißensee Cemetery Fund"
Bradford, England ermöglicht.
1992

Plaque on Weißensee Cemetery, Berlin, commemorating its clean-up by Rudi. "The erection of this plaque was made possible by a donation from the Weißensee Cemetery Fund, Bradford, England 1992."

The gate to Birkenau concentration camp, part of Auschwitz.
Note the inverted 'B' in 'Arbeit': Polish prisoners who were forced to
construct it realised the obscene lie and inserted a deliberate mistake.
Translation: 'Work sets you free'.

TO ENGLAND…

My father had travelled to 'England' five times, my mother three times trying to obtain entry visas. When eventually they had them, my father then had to get permission to work. When the clerk handed him the certificate enabling him to do so he said he could work anywhere except London and Manchester. My father said, 'Where can I work?' The clerk metaphorically stuck a pin into a map of England and as Bradford lay fairly centrally, he said 'go to Bradford'. My father jumped on the next train there where fortunately there was a relative of my mother's, who introduced him to a wool merchant Harry Kramrisch who did a lot of trade with Yugoslavia. They made him Consul which enabled him to have access to diplomatic bags which, when sealed, could be transported across country borders without being opened by the customs. He suggested to my father that he should place valuables in a parcel, take it to the Yugoslav embassy in Berlin with the request to send it to the embassy in London, which he did and which they did. On his next visit to London he went to the embassy and collected his parcel. When we eventually arrived in Bradford my first friend was Fay Kramrisch, granddaughter of Harry and at 94 she is still my friend. As she now lives in a care home and can only get out if someone takes her out, I do that once a week when I take her for lunch. I would do it anyway but if ever there were a realisation of the proverb 'one good turn deserves another' this would be it, albeit after an interval of 82 years.

On their last visit to Bradford before emigration they had paid a deposit on a house in near-by Shipley, telling the current owners that we would be back to claim residence in early November 1937. However, when we knocked on the door the incumbents were still in residence, forcing us to spend a week in a residential hotel, eating up precious money earmarked for other anticipated expenditure. To add to a bad situation my mother developed a very painful inner ear infection which the doctor, also a refugee (so discussion could take place in German), treated as best he could without, of course, the benefit of antibiotics, yet to be discovered.

At last we could move in. Our furniture had arrived in large wooden boxes called lifts which were shipped across the ocean. We were so lucky to have been able to take all our possessions with us. Later refugees were lucky to escape with their lives and nothing else whilst six million did not even escape with their lives.

There was no central heating and hot water was produced by a 'back boiler' in the kitchen. Heating in rooms was open coal fires or, later, electric radiators. As my mother was going to help my father in the surgery a maid called Daisy Little was engaged to do the housework.

We made contact with the local rabbi of the orthodox Synagogue, Rev. Jacob Israelstam. My parents must have discussed schooling with him for they decided that I should go to the best school in town, Bradford Grammar (BGS). It was not a free school, a term costing £7 which was a large sum in those days by any standards but must have been a considerable drain on the family's finances. Mrs. Elsie Israelstam took my mother and me to see the headmaster. I took my leaving report. The German system of marks for work done is by the numbers 1 – 5, 1 being excellent, 5 very poor. Having always been a fairly good pupil I had lots of 1's and 2's. What the Headmaster thought of such low numerical marks in the British system of marking we shall never know, but he accepted me. I had learnt English at the German school for 18 months, so soon found my feet. Paradoxically as English was still a foreign language for me, I mastered syntax and grammar more easily than the local boys (in those days it was a single sex school) and soon reached the top of the class to applause. However, my language skills let me down when a note came to the class telling me to go to the headmaster's study. He enquired very kindly how I was getting on. I told him that I thought I was fine. He complemented me and dismissed me. On returning to the class the master said, 'Did you get the cane?' because that was the usual reason for being sent to the head. Still beaming across my whole face at the head's kindness but not knowing what the word 'cane' meant, I said 'yes, sir'. The whole class erupted into fits of laughter, realising what the situation was. To help me integrate into the school l went to the geography master, Mr. Herbert Clarke of BGS, for more lessons in English language and ethos. He was a very refined man, a true gentleman as I was able to judge even at my early age. He later became headmaster of the only secondary school in the country for blind children in Worcester. I owe him a lot for what he did for me.

At the beginning of the next school year I was put into the classical stream, learning Latin and Greek both of which I loved, more for vocabulary, syntax and grammar (again!) than the set books which were translated laboriously line by line, thus losing any continuity and broader picture. It was this literature that pulled me down, I am sure, from a distinction to a credit in the 'School Certificate' (called GCSE in 2018) examination three years later. However, I had the distinction of having been awarded the highest marks in any subject for any pupil in the school for German, no particular surprise as it was after all my mother-tongue. I then had to change to the science side to study physics and chemistry if I was going to study dentistry later. Unfortunately, I lacked the groundwork for these subjects and nobody had thought to tell the relevant masters, so that from being near the top of the class in most subjects I became the dunce. This had a detrimental effect educationally and emotionally, forcing my parents to arrange coaching lessons for me. One of these teachers was a family friend, Peter Wohlfarth, who became a world authority on 'Magnetism'. Note: I had two friends who were world authorities in their subjects! Reflected glory! Peter's father Paul was a judge in Breslau, Germany, now called Wroclaw (in Poland) where Marianne and her parents came from, but he could not exercise his profession in England.

Father in Bradford in the 1960s

Mother in Bradford in the 1960s

AND SO, TO UNIVERSITY

Fortunately, there was a dramatic piece of luck. Halfway through the second year of senior school my father visited the professor of dentistry at Leeds University to ascertain requirements for entry on to a course. It appears that there was quite a discussion involving aspects of dentistry in Germany at the end of which the professor told my father to send 'him', meaning myself, to visit him for interview. I had no idea what he was going to ask me. The conversation went like this: 'Are you good with your hands?' 'Not particularly.' 'Can you build model aeroplanes?' 'No.' 'Can you build model cars?' 'No.' When he realised that he was not getting any further with practicalities he changed the subject. 'Which books did you read for school certificate?' 'Julius Caesar.' 'What did Mark Anthony say at Caesar's funeral?' 'Friends, Romans, countrymen, lend me your ears. I come to bury Caesar, not to praise him. The evil that men do lives after them, the good is oft interred with their bones...' At that point he said 'stop', which was just as well because I did not know any further. And he said, 'start in September.' Further luck was that I had not even taken the Higher School Certificate at that time, let alone pass it. In fact, I failed it, getting only subsidiary marks and poor ones at that. The curse of having been a poor pupil pursued me for the whole of my University studies – I could not shake off the bane of being bottom of the class. I failed the examination in metallurgy which, however, did not prevent me from continuing with the course, having been told that I could retake this examination whenever I wanted. I procrastinated this from one year to the next and when the time came to sit my finals, I realised that I had yet to take the metallurgy examination. This proved especially irksome, but I obviously managed it 'mit ach und krach' (with great difficulty).

In addition, I spent much time on music presenting gramophone recitals during lunchtimes in the students' union building twice a week, which needed preparation. The 'gramophone' had two turntables and pieces of music which spread over more than three sides of the records which, in those days, played for no more than 4 ½ minutes maximum at 78 revolutions per minute, were arranged in 'automatic couplings', which meant that in a piece of music lasting over four records, sides 1 to 4 would be spread over four records and sides 5 to 8 would be spread over the reverse sides. If sides 1 and 2 were placed on the adjacent turntables when the music finished on side 1 it could be continued on side 2 seamlessly. Unfortunately, the music on the next side of different records did not always start at the same time from the beginning of the record and each changeover had to be practiced until it was perfect and listeners would not be able to detect when the changeover happened. All this was time-consuming at the expense of learning my lessons. Also, when I did my coursework at home, I would usually have the radio 'on', especially when a piece of music was played which I had not heard before or one that was a particular favourite. Thus, I learned a lot of music but failed most of the examinations at least twice, much to my parents' sorrow and mine. When I passed my finals in 1943, I vowed never to take another examination.

However, the vow was broken in pleasurable circumstances about which more later. I had also joined the University orchestra, becoming leader of the second violins, and the University quartet with whom I gave only one concert – a Schubert quartet. I had of course attended several rehearsals but had to miss the dress rehearsal at which the other three had to decide whether to observe a particular repeat. They did decide but forgot to inform me. When it came to the place in the music, I did not know whether to play the repeat or not: it was a 50-50 decision. Fortunately, I chose the right one.

At this students' union I also occasionally invited musicians to give a lunchtime talk. So, Maurice Miles (conductor of the then resident Yorkshire Symphony Orchestra), Sir Charles Groves, Alec Robertson (BBC broadcaster) and Alan Rawsthorne (eminent composer), came. I had arranged to meet Rawsthorne at the train station and another man was equally waiting. We got into conversation and he turned out to be Ernest Bradbury, recently appointed music critic of the Yorkshire Post. He was also meeting Rawsthorne and it was his first outside engagement. We remained good friends for the time he spent in office.

In those days the local orchestra was the Northern Philharmonic Orchestra composed 50/50 of professionals and (very good) amateurs. But it was not quite good enough to hold its own with fully professional orchestras. So, Leeds City Council founded the Yorkshire Symphony Orchestra with support from 10 or so local councils. Their conductor was Maurice Miles who had worked a lot in London and for the BBC and who, in my estimation, was very good. But for a variety of reasons the money tended to dry up and Leeds decided to employ an internationally known conductor,

Nicolai Malko, to succeed Miles in the hope of reviving the orchestra's fortunes. However, that did not do the trick either and the finances found themselves short of £35k which even in those days, for an orchestra, was not a huge sum, but Leeds City Council to their shame disbanded the orchestra forthwith.

My parents had befriended a young couple, Arthur and Kathleen Barker. Arthur played the violin and Kathleen the piano; both played exceedingly well. They often came to our house and usually played through all the classical violin concertos on successive evenings with a perfect technique and that is how I got know these musical gems very well. They had one son and moved south where most tragically the son was murdered when in his late teens. The couple emigrated to Cape Town, South Africa, where Arthur joined the South African Symphony Orchestra.

Through turning pages for my father playing the piano I learnt to read music but only as written for piano. My first exposure to orchestral music was from the film 'Robin Hood', and later became more consciously aware of music other than piano music. My first such experience was inevitably the overture to Rossini's 'Barber of Seville'; the second, most adventurously, Liszt's first piano concerto in E flat. I realised that the players must play from notes, went to the library and enquired. They produced an orchestral score of this music which I took home and studied intimately and soon I was subsumed into a world of orchestral music through radio, records and scores that took up every spare minute.

Every year the students arranged a 'Rag Week' consisting of social functions, dances, concerts, etc. I decided that I would arrange a symphony concert sanctioned by the committee. Well in advance of the proposed dates I approached Maurice Miles and an internationally known pianist Shulamith Shafir. Both consented to perform even leaving it to me to choose the programme, providing it was in their current repertoire: Tchaikovsky's First Piano Concerto (to draw the crowds), Brahms' Fourth Symphony and two shorter pieces. It was certainly an artistic success.

Students put on a reading of James Elroy Flecker's book 'Hassan' for which they invited me to choose music (on records). At the end of the book was a reference to the town of Samarkand and in the context it assumed an iconic flavour, instilling in me a desire to visit this place. The opportunity came many years later when we booked a trip to Uzbekistan, an unworldly place it seemed to us. But Samarkand was a fascinating town with a huge number of historical buildings; going on then to nearby Bukhara. Here we found two bazaars on opposite sides of the road where we saw a beautiful rug in each. We wanted to buy only one and oscillated between the two several times not being able to make up our mind which one to acquire, the sales ladies each saying to themselves 'please let it be me.' Eventually we chose one. This episode was repeated when we wanted to buy a wall embroidery in Mexico when two ladies standing next to each other held up their respective pieces and we looked at one, then the other several times until eventually choosing one.

After qualifying I spent six months postgraduate study at the Eastman Clinic in London supplementing my meagre earnings of £7 a week by working in general practice in a surgery in Golders Green where I stayed as a lodger with my sister Winnie. My name was still Librowicz, not to be changed till much later. The dentist for whom I worked thought the name was too difficult for his patients and suggested that I be called Lee. One of my patients was a BBC producer who said that he would give me a couple of free tickets for one of his shows. It suited both of us that he would drop them in at the Eastman Clinic, but I heard no more about it. Many weeks later I happened to speak to a colleague called Lee at the Clinic who told me that he had received an envelope addressed to him with some BBC tickets!

Living in London enabled me to attend concerts and the opera frequently. The Royal Festival Hall had recently been opened for the 1951 Festival, which was intended to lift the country out of its exhaustion of winning the war. I always envied the performers on stage at this venue or the Royal Albert Hall. I also joined the Youth Group attached to the Reform Synagogue in Alyth Gardens where I was soon voted on to the committee – the first step on always being on some committee or other. I was joint member of a subcommittee to design a badge for the YASGB (Youth Association of Synagogue of Great Britain) and gave a talk on the grammar of music illustrating it on the piano by playing excerpts from Glazunov's Fifth Symphony.

NATIONAL SERVICE

I received my call-up papers for the army as the country had compulsory national service whereby every able-bodied man had to serve two years in one of the forces. Fortunately, I could join as a dental surgeon. Between the six months in London and joining up I attended a youth conference in Glasgow, travelling back to Bradford on Easter Monday. I had to find out if the train service was a bank holiday or normal one. At the station enquiry desk, the clerk in a loud voice (with a room full of Scots people) said, 'Where are you going? England?' The reason for the question was that trains within Scotland had a different timetable from those going to England.

I was posted to Aldershot for a six weeks' induction course, then was sent to a small army camp nearby called Cove. During my stay in the officers' mess one of the first colour television sets was purchased. One day a beautiful spider's web complete with spider was spotted across a window. A fly was caught by some of us and thrown into the web causing the spider to travel along its web at an amazing speed to envelop the poor fly in thread. It was to see this spectacle that we set the murder up. We felt guilty but were enriched by seeing at close quarters what was happening in nature all the time. One evening my comrades asked for a volunteer to be hypnotised as one of them said he could 'do it'. Sitting comfortably on a chair he did actually succeed in hypnotising me. I felt as if I were floating in space. He asked me to hold my hand out palm downwards and proceeded to waft a lit cigarette lighter slowly to and fro under my fingers and, knowing full well what he was doing, I only felt a slight warmth where ordinarily I would have winced with pain. He duly 'brought me round' again.

Cove was near London, so most weekends I went there to stay first with my great-uncle Hugo, brother of my grandmother who was an absolute image of Winston Churchill, and his wife Betty, then later with Betty's brother-in-law, Sasha. He did not have milk in the flat, so I had to have my breakfast drink without milk and still drink tea neat. I continued to attend concerts and opera, catching the last train and bus back.

In order not to stagnate in the evenings I usually went to the education centre where I met two people who would 'make it' in later adult life: another dental surgeon, Wilfred Josephs, from Newcastle, was a musician composing in his spare time. When I met him some time later, he told me that he took lessons from Nadia Boulanger, the Paris-based very famous composition teacher, having pawned his wife's engagement ring to pay for lessons. Inter alia he wrote the music for the TV drama 'I, Claudius'. Sadly, he died very young. The other was Myer Fredman who had a degree in music. He became chorus master at Glyndebourne. His luck was in when John Barbirolli who had been engaged to conduct the Hallé Orchestra in Japan died suddenly and John Pritchard, who then conducted at Glyndebourne, was asked to step in at short notice, so Myer stepped into conducting at Glyndebourne. I approached him to get me two tickets which were very difficult to obtain (against payment, of course) and which he did. This visit was quite an adventure. Glyndebourne had a tiny railway station which was only functional when the opera season was on. Passengers on the train from Victoria were all in evening dress and we had the obligatory picnic on the lawn in the interval. I think we saw *Eugene Onegin* by Tchaikovsky. Sometime later Glyndebourne Opera came to Leeds, before the days of Opera North, and we renewed our acquaintance. He became conductor of orchestras in New Zealand and Australia..

After a year I was transferred to Austria, travelling there by a special troop train called Medloc (Mediterranean lines of communication). Fortunately, I had a sleeper compartment to myself. Whilst the train was standing in Munich station by chance the train standing on the neighbouring track had its destination sign right opposite my window. It said 'Dachau'. This was the first time that I came face to face with the name of a concentration camp in black and white. It was 1954 and the horrors of the Holocaust, for whatever reason, were not discussed and knowledge about it and them was scant. I assume the reason was that it was realised that the subject would be most painful and distressing, therefor the world was not yet ready to face it. So, the sight of this destination plate was most disturbing more than I can describe in words. I became quite disorientated and it was fortunate that I was alone in the compartment. In that train I could see people reading the paper, smoking, talking about everyday matters. Did they not appreciate that the train and they were going to what had been a death machine? I was glad when Medloc pulled out of the station and that dreaded word was out of sight.

When the train arrived in Villach in deep snow there was an announcement over the loudspeaker system that everybody except Lt. Librowicz was to detrain on the left. The reason for that was that I was being met by the dental officer (as we were called in the army) whom I was relieving, and this was the easiest way to meet me.

I was very happy in Austria. I was a 'mobile' dentist, spending a few months in Villach, Klagenfurth, Zeltweg, where the dental suite was on the top floor of the control tower of a disused airport, Graz, Spital, Vienna and freeport Trieste, now part of Italy. Richard Strauss' last opera *'Die Liebe der Danae'* was being given its first performance in Salzburg. With great difficulty I bought a ticket and having obtained permission to leave early, caught a train from Spital to Salzburg. Halfway there the train stopped with the explanation that a goods train ahead had derailed. Thinking that such could not be remedied in a hurry I was able to send a telegram to the theatre to say that my ticket could be sold. However, the derailment was put right sooner than I thought possible and I arrived in Salzburg half an hour after the beginning of the opera. As luck would have it walking along the road from the station to the theatre, I was able to hear the music from one loudspeaker after the other where restaurants along the road were relaying the broadcast from the theatre to diners eating in the gardens. As my ticket had not been sold, I was able to see the second half.

Many years later when we holidayed in Badgastein we went to Salzburg to see *'Jedermann'* by Hugo von Hoffmannsthal in the open air. This was very impressive.

In 1946 my parents had bought their first car – a second-hand pre-war Ford 10. This was now 10 years old and its biggest handicap was that it was difficult to start and, in that case, had to be started with a cranking handle which was standard issue on all cars. New cars were being directed for export to earn foreign currency and one had to put one's name down for a new car and wait up to a number of years, so when the chance of a new car came along, having reached the top of the waiting-list whilst I was in the army my parents bought it and were now the owners of two cars. In typical generosity they saved it for me for when I was demobilised from the army. This lasted me until 1963 when I changed it for a Citroen DS model whose shape and suspension intrigued me. It was also the time of the rise of the Beatles. I remained faithful to Citroen especially when they introduced a model with three tip-up seats between the front and rear seats, which was ideal for when we had first three, then four children. Later we had a Peugeot with a similar layout of seats, then back to a Citroen until a relatively minor repair cost a lot of money and with the steep rise in the cost of petrol downgraded to a smaller car. In between I drove on LPG (liquefied petroleum gas) which caught on in a big way in some mainland European countries but not here. After the initial expense of having the system fitted LPG was a lot cheaper than petrol or diesel. In some cars I also had a system fitted which would keep the accelerator at a certain pitch automatically without having to keep the foot on the pedal which was very useful on long motorway journeys. A touch on the brake pedal would immediately disengage it.

Surviving the Holocaust

One survivor of our Family was great-aunt Hulda my grandmother's sister, who had only been married for two years, then parted childless. She survived Theresienstadt (in Czech Terezin). She was deported there together with my grandmother, Bertha. My grandmother died there presumably of hunger, cold and disease. It is a debatable point whether a person who died of hunger, etc., was not actually murdered. Some people would say that they were as murdered as if they had been shot or gassed. In Terezin the bodies were usually cremated and the ashes thrown into the river. Whilst on a short holiday in Prague we took a local bus to visit this camp and met the person in charge who had himself been a prisoner there during the war. He invited us into his office where he showed us books which contained the names of all the people who were imprisoned there, including my grandmother's and great-aunt's names. Many people were forcibly put on trains to Auschwitz where they were usually gassed. One day news came that people could volunteer to be transported to Switzerland and freedom. This came about because of an agreement between the Americans and Germans that the Americans would provide the Germans with gold against the release of Jewish prisoners. The American money was donated by Jews. Now the inmates did not know whether this was a trick or not and those who accepted entered into a proper gamble. Only when they saw glistening pristine Swiss railway coaches within the camp did they realise that it was for real and about 1000 Jewish people were literally rescued from Terezin and taken to Engelberg. Hulda relates that among the food they were given on the train by friendly staff was a rosy apple. In the camp food tended to be hoarded rather than eaten and it was quite a while though she was hungry before she ate it. Hulda lived with us until her natural death in 1955 and not once did we question her about life in the camp. That was obviously because we did not want to distress her, but it would have given us an insight into personal recollections and conditions in the camp.

When Hulda learnt after the war that several family members had died in the Holocaust, including four-year-old Dan she wrote the following poem:

'Es fiel ein Reif in der Frühlingsluft, mein süsser Bub, wer
        hätte das gedacht
Dass Du durch Mörderhand bist umgebracht?
Du warst mein Alles, warst mein Glück und Stern,
Nur Gott allein es weiss, wie hatte ich Dich so gern.
Verhallt sind Deine Schritte, verstummt Dein süsser Mund,
Es gab für mich nichts Schöneres im ganzen Erdenrund.
Verjüngtest mir die Jahre, brachtest Sonne ringsumher,
Ich kann es garnicht fassen, das jetzt ist alles leer.
Nie wieder soll ich sehen Dein liebes Angesicht,
Gott wollt' noch einen Engel und so rief er Dich.
Ich träumt' von schöneren Tagen, hofft' auf ein
        Wiedersehen,
Der Traum ist nun verronnen, ich muss alleine gehen.
Ewig werd' ich um Dich weinen, bis der Tod mich wird mit
        Dir vereinen'.

Translation:

'There was a frost that spring night, my dear sweet boy,
whoever would have thought
You could be murdered in this way! You were my
everything, my happiness,
The apple of my eye, God alone knows how I loved you.
Stifled are your steps,
Silenced your sweet mouth, for me nothing in the world was
more beautiful.
You made the years young for me, brought sunlight all
around. I cannot grasp
How empty everything is now. Never again will I see your
beloved face.
God wanted one more angel and He created you. I dreamt
of better days,
Hoped we'll meet again, that dream now is past, I must go
alone.
I will weep for you for ever till death will bring us together.'

Translated by the Association of Jewish refugees (AJR)

Visit to Auschwitz-Birkenau 1999

Having visited Theresienstadt (Terezin) where my grandmother died, and Sachsenhausen (Oranianberg) concentration camps I wanted to see for myself the nadir of the camps where seven of our relatives, including Dan aged four, had died.

A closed Jewish party of 232 people from the north of England flew from Manchester to Krakow, then flew back all in the same day.

Even when I saw the preliminary invitation with the word at its head, it sent the proverbial shivers up and down my spine. On site, nothing that I had read or heard prepared me for the horror of what I saw.

The camp is in two parts, Auschwitz 1 and Birkenau, about two kilometers away. Both were surrounded by triple length of once electrified barbed wire. A local guide, very pleasant and knowledgeable, but with an expressionless face, took us through an entrance which used to be the actual reception area for prisoners (as a good friend of ours who was one such called himself). A modern sign warned that children under 14 should not be taken round the camp. Originally people who were opponents of the state – gypsies, some Catholics and homosexuals – would go to Auschwitz 1; only later were Jews also transported there. Accommodation was in barracks. These now housed photographs, paintings, copies of documents appertaining to the Holocaust, but also large vitrines of spectacles, hair, artificial limbs, shoes and clothes including children's, dummies, hairbrushes, shaving brushes, tins of shoe polish, pots and pans, chamber pots and tallitim (prayer shawls): these were all belongings of prisoners who were killed, but those effects were utilized e.g. hair was woven into blankets, as was proved by analysing such blankets after the war when they showed human hair; clothes were sent to Germany for poor people etc. There must have been thousands of articles like shoes. One window showed hundreds of suitcases on which the prisoners had been ordered to paint in large white letters their name and their hometown so that they could reclaim them after their shower (see below). All these artefacts were stored in a hut called 'Canada', this being the symbol of wealth and prosperity. After the war some blankets whose weave included human hair were analysed and traces of gas were found in them.

One barrack house, the punishment block, had a cell which had held Father Maximillian Kolbe who took the place of another man who had four children, for execution. Another block had Stehzellen (stand-up cells) which were small bricked-in enclosures, into which four prisoners were packed and left for up to 24 hours, but there was only room for them to stand. Just around the corner from this block was a rectangular area with a brick wall at the end which was the death wall, where prisoners were shot sometimes for the most minor infringement of rules.

Another block showed artefacts like newspapers of the period. One such was 'Der Stürmer' with headlines: Nürnberg November 1938 – Keine Judenanwälte mehr (No more Jewish lawyers). The fact that eventually most prisoners in Auschwitz were Jews was played down by the

Polish Government which now administered the camp site; one room in this block had a large Hebrew inscription on the wall, a small crypt with Jewish symbols and provision for a Hebrew lament to be heard on tape, sung by a one-time prisoner. Food for prisoners would consist of a mugful of Ersatzkaffee (artificial coffee) for breakfast, half a litre of thin soup with small bits of meat a few times a week for lunch and stale bread and a tiny bit of margarine for supper. A rudimentary map, with Auschwitz at its centre, was drawn since the war showing inter alia Inowrazlaw, where my father's family came from, and Wrozlaw, formerly Breslau, where Marianne's family came from.

Over one of the 'avenues' was a metal girder bridge with the obscene motto 'Arbeit macht frei' 'Work sets you free'. It was interesting to note that the B in 'ARBEIT' is inverted, i.e. the large loop is on top of the smaller loop. I learnt later that Polish prisoners were forced to construct this sign, noticed that it showed a grotesque lie and decided to introduce a deliberate mistake.

Next on the tour were the gas chambers and furnaces. Prisoners would be told to undress in order for them to 'take a shower' as part of the disinfectant process. A hundred or more were then herded into a large room, the door was locked behind them and crystals of Zyklon B allowed to fall into the room through special openings in the ceiling. When the crystals fell to the ground and lay there, they would give off poisonous gas which would kill the prisoners within a few minutes. The doors would be opened; anybody seen to be moving would be shot with a pistol. The bodies would be loaded on to carts and taken to metal skips like underground coal trucks. These ran on rails with points, turntables and cross rails, so that the skips could be positioned directly in front of furnaces. Sometimes there were so many corpses that the furnaces could not cope and the bodies were dumped outside and burned. A factory near Frankfurt which manufactured Zyklon B gas was bombed and there was a temporary scarcity of gas, so prisoners were 'simply' shot, according to the guide.

In front of one of the barracks was a (reconstructed) gallows, on which prisoners who tried to escape or those who helped an escapee, were hanged and everybody had to attend to watch. A few yards further was another gallows on which the camp commandant Höss was himself hanged after the war.

Substantial numbers of prisoners were killed on arrival without any registration, depending on whether they looked capable for work, whether the camp was full and on the whim of the SS officer doing the selection. There were photographs of arrivals on railway platforms where such selections took place.

As we walked around emotions ran high. As one horror after another was revealed, the mind could eventually no longer absorb and digest the absolute subhuman behavior of their perpetrators. Not content with abusing the prisoners and killing them, they were taunted and bullied, families torn asunder without a chance for them to say farewell, children were torn from their parents. And all this without proper food, water or sanitation. Our emotions ran over.

Numbed we were bussed to Birkenau where worse was to come. A special railway branch line had been built from the main line direct into the camp underneath a watchtower. Once inside the line branched out into three, with a half-mile long platform between two of them. On arrival of a train the doors of the goods wagons, into which up to 70 or so people had been herded and packed tightly, were opened. Those still alive were lined up in two rows, men in one and women and children in the other, and a SS doctor decided with the movement of a riding whip whether a prisoner had to go to the left or the right, depending, again, on whether he/she was fit for work or not. If they were fit for work, they were led to barracks, if not they were herded direct to gas chambers and crematoria without the slightest chance of families saying good-bye to one another.The ashes were thrown into three shallow pools, which happened to be near the ovens, and they contain such ashes to this day. Those who had died on the train journey were taken to the crematoria.

Those who ended up in the barracks were welcomed by the commandant who said that the only way out from here was through the chimneys of the furnaces. Yet starvation was the single largest killer. To the right there were about 50 rectangular barracks. One of these had a stone table running along its centre on which prisoners ate, sat, slept and bore babies. Another had a long wooden platform with holes for toilet functions, two rows alongside each other, the holes in one row being in the gaps of the other row. All prisoners suffered from digestive problems but were only allowed to use the toilets twice a day. For 60 or so sitters there would be no privacy whatsoever, no water and no paper. The intellectuals among them were designated to clean out the latrines so as to humiliate them. To the left was another group of barracks. Between this on the one hand and the railway lines and platform on the other were the ruins of perhaps 20 furnaces and their chimneys, so the prisoners saw where they would eventually end up each and every day.

Prisoners had learnt that if there were no fleas on a person, that person was dead. When the camp was liberated one of the actions was to de-louse the prisoners, but they could not accept that they had no insects, so they would capture an errant flea and wrap it in folded paper and release it on themselves to prove to themselves that they were still alive, so ingrained in them was the foible.

A series of memorial stones now stand at the end of the complex. The nearby gas chambers had been hastily blown up by the Germans as the Russians advanced from the east in 1945 but the ruins remain in situ.

Rabbi Barry Marcus of London, who accompanied the group, after appropriate prayers, made a moving speech saying, inter alia, that for a day we had put our daily lives on hold to wander around the site of the most depraved atrocities ever committed. And yet we could not comprehend the depth of such subhuman behavior, perpetrated here and in five other death camps, though there were up to 100 concentration camps.

At the exact point on the railway platform now looking clean and tidy, where prisoners were motioned to go to the left, for a probably short lease of life, or to the right directly to the gas chambers, I lit my candle and sang the Hebrew mourning song, reciting within it the names of our relatives, who passed this spot under different circumstances 56 years ago. As I walked away along the rails stepping from sleeper to sleeper my mind was numb, an absolute blank, unable to think any useful thoughts or any thoughts, useful or not..

If this is an emotional account no excuse is made, for it could not be otherwise.

For further reading: 'Auschwitz, 1270 to the present' by Deborah Dwork and Robert Jan van Pelt pub.

1996 by V. V. Norton & Co, New York and London

THE FATE OF FAMILY AND FRIENDS

Relatives who were murdered in Auschwitz were Evi, daughter of the youngest sister of my paternal grandmother, her husband Werner, her four-year-old son Dan, her father Arthur, Hannush, a sister of the same grandmother, and her two unmarried daughters Else and Hedwig. My father had obtained permission from the Home Office for these two to come to England, but only as domestic servants (which was the usual arrangement for single ladies in a certain age bracket) but they refused to come under those conditions. Tragically they paid the ultimate price for their refusal. Marianne's maternal grandmother Edith and an uncle died but I don't know in which camp.

On this daytrip from Manchester to Krakow, especially in a Jewish group, the usual loud discussion, if not plain banter, ensued on the flight out. On the return journey there was a palpably profound silence, broken only by joint prayers which in itself was moving. Never has the mourner's *kaddish* been recited with more devotion and tears.

Grandmother Bertha had more sisters and a brother Hugo who lived in Stettin and was married to Betty. He was a philatelist, lover of music and of good food, becoming a good image of Winston Churchill. They had no children. A story is told that Betty had prepared a chicken and to keep it fresh before the days of refrigerators hung it on the balcony overnight. Hugo wanted to taste it and cut a bit off and later cut another bit off and again. By morning there was nothing left. They emigrated to London. When during the war London was much bombed, they asked if they could stay with us. When their train stopped at Bedford and later Retford, where porters shouted out the names of the stations as signs were prohibited, they thought both times they had arrived at Bradford. Unmarried sisters were Cäzilie and 'Etta' who lost a leg in a car accident. When Jews were rounded up to be transported to the East, she committed suicide. A married sister was Hannah (Hannush) who married a namesake, Jakob Marcus. They had two daughters Else and Hedwig (see above), Jakob having died of prostate cancer earlier. The youngest sister of my grandmother, Frederike nicknamed Trulle, married Arthur Blumenthal who owned three hardware shops which prospered. He bought a whole block of flats in one of which my grandmother, Hulda and the three other sisters lived.

Trulle and Arthur had two daughters: Ruth, who married Simcha Kamm and emigrated to Palestine in 1934 where they had three daughters: Dani, Noomi and Chawa. Chawa married Michael Dror, had two children Ron and Daphna and emigrated to the USA. They first lived in Salt Lake City, home of the Mormons and on a visit to them we went to the site of the Mormons and where their founder Josef Smith, coming from the East coast to seek new pasture, first saw the area and exclaimed 'this is the land'. The reason why Mormons were allowed to marry more than one wife was that on their travels they had often to fight their way through hostile areas and lost many men producing an inequality of numbers of women and men. It appears that this has now stabilised and one wife is again the norm. The nearby lake called Saltair suffered a storm and presumably a local earthquake, which raised the level of the water by several feet half drowning a house by the shore making it permanently uninhabitable. (A suburb of Bradford is called Saltaire after Sir Titus Salt who built a woollen mill next to the river Aire and is a UNESCO historical site.) They then moved to Denver, and, after the children married and had children, themselves moved to the West coast.

Ruth's younger sister Evi or Eva lived with her parents in one of the other flats of Arthur's house and whilst my parents paid several visits to England to try to obtain permission for immigration, I often stayed with them, my sister Winnie staying with the Stimmings. Evi then 19 or so was very good looking and for all of my 11 years slightly fell in love with her. Arthur was one of the first to own a large black car and Evi could drive it which raised her even further in my estimation and admiration. After our emigration Evi married Werner Simon and they had Dan. Evi paid a visit to Palestine to see her sister Ruth. It appears that she did not have the correct papers for a prolonged visit and therefore would have become an illegal visitor. Even so her sister tried to persuade her to stay permanently but she decided to return to her husband and child. In 1944 she, her husband, father Arthur and Dan were deported to Auschwitz where they were murdered. I like to think that, as a child's sentience does not begin until about four years of age, he would not have known what was going on. The same could most tragically not be said of his parents and grandfather who would know only too well what was going on, nor of Aunt Hannush and her daughters Else and Hede. Fortunately, one of my grandchildren is called Daniel. Their thoughts in the gas chamber are unimaginable. Dani's husband Gideon became manager in charge of all telephone service in Southern Israel. When I visited Israel the first time, they took me on a tourist trip round Tel Aviv and showed me a recently opened department store Diezengoff which had an alcove with 12 public telephones (before the age of mobile 'phones), and a money changing machine. As we stood and watched a man had inserted some money and waited for his change, but none came. He resorted to all sorts of antics and in frustration turned round and addressed the nearest person who was Gideon in uncomplimentary terms. Gideon made no reply and explained later that though he was responsible for the telephones he was not responsible for the money-changing machine.

 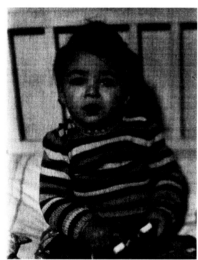

Evi (Eva), murdered in Auschwitz.   *My cousin Dan (son of Evi) who*
Photo circa 1942   *perished in Auschwitz at age four*

CULTURAL AND RELIGIOUS LIFE

In Berlin my parents' best friends were arguably the Bandows. Frederik, nicknamed Fifa, was a judge at the Ministry of Finance; his wife Margarete, nicknamed Marga, played the piano, violin and viola. They were also one of the first to own a car – an Adler. Marga gave me piano lessons but, though I liked playing, I did not like practicing and having learnt to play a piece would continue to play it by heart, i.e. not looking at the notes, which in itself would not be a bad achievement but it retarded my sight-reading and playing. Lack of practicing prevented progress and my parents thought if I tried another instrument I would possibly succeed. Again, though I liked the violin, I did not practice and much later, when we had settled in Bradford, we got acquainted with a young couple, as mentioned before: Arthur played the violin very well, later playing in the South Africa Symphony Orchestra in Cape Town, and his wife Kathleen who played the piano very well. They often came to our house and played all the classical violin concertos. He gave me lessons but again I did not practice and I eventually stopped them. But that did not dampen my love of music.

The Bandows had three sons: Eberhardt who was strong like Esau in the Old Testament (OT); Heini who was the intellectual like Jacob (OT) and Klaus – one for the ladies. Eberhardt became an engineer, married Irmgard and had

Gisela and later died very young of liver cancer. Heini was killed in the war in Italy just before its end and his final whereabouts has never been established. Klaus married Erika and they had two children, Christian and Claudia. Klaus became spokesman for BMW in Munich. He died in 2017 aged 95.

My father was a very good pianist. His playing when I was very young and still in a state of absorbing music in all its ramifications, appeared normal to me – this is as it should be: only in retrospect when I realised the complexities of playing any instrument did I come to the conclusion that my father's playing was really excellent. Where he took the time to practice for him to become so proficient, I do not know for he also studied Jewish history keenly in which he was also very knowledgeable. I used to turn the pages for him and thus learned to read music. He used to play all the solo repertoire of Chopin, Schubert pieces, Beethoven sonatas, etc.

Following my singing success in Berlin with Loewy, once in England my parents took me to concerts in Bradford where a long tradition ensured 12 visits a year by the Manchester based Hallé Orchestra. They had lost their permanent conductor Sir Hamilton Harty and fortunately were able to engage the best conductors on an ad hoc basis like Sir Henry Wood and Sir Thomas Beecham until John Barbirolli was enticed to return to England from the New York Philharmonic Orchestra. One concert led to a peculiar occurrence: I had long had a fascination with fugues and one piece – *Variations and Fugue on a Theme of Mozart* by Max Reger – had a fantastic fugue at the end (shall I say in magnificent technicolour – to mix metaphors). After the interval came Tchaikovsky's Sixth Symphony, the *Pathetique*, which I knew well and liked a lot. However, after the Rheinberger, whose fugue put me on an emotional 'high', I just could not face it and told my parents that I was going home which did not go down well with my mother. But attending so many concerts I got to know many pieces of music very well and started collecting records and borrowing scores (printed music) from the library and learnt to follow an orchestral score which opened a new world for me. There were also Music Club concerts where a pianist or chamber group would perform. Again, the finest artists of the day came. In the beginning I was fairly naïve and when on the programme for a piano recital it said at the end 'Steinway – piano' I asked who this composer Steinway was.

I saw my first film when I was about eight when my mother, who really was the one who wanted to go to the newly 'discovered' cinema, took me with her to see Shirley Temple who was then the child star in everybody's vocabulary. We were duly impressed by this wonderful invention of moving pictures. Then at age of about 12, I saw my first film in England: it was *'Robin Hood'* with Errol Flynn. In those days many cinemas had continuous performances where the complete programme – main feature, news, cartoon (starting midday and continuing until late evening) – was repeated. I sat through two and a half cycles, not being able to tear myself away. This was partly because I had never seen such a film before and it was even in retrospect very good and still talked about. It was years later that I tumbled to another reason why I sat through it again and again: I had never heard such accompanying music. Erich Korngold, who, being Jewish, had left Vienna, had come to Hollywood much to his and their advantage, and had written a wonderful score for full symphony orchestra. This was a new and fascinating sound to me and I just could not tear myself away. I came home late much to the concern of my parents, but I had discovered, unknowingly, symphonic music. My next exposure to symphonic music came unexpectedly when we went to the cinema not really knowing what it was all about. It concerned the preparation and performance of a concert at Tanglewood, a suburb of Boston, USA. The climax was a partial performance of Grieg's Piano Concerto played by a young very good-looking girl. The music was a revelation to me and I must have fallen in love not only with the music but with the pianist. A combination of the two made a most agreeable impression on a youngster in his early teens whose hormones were just awakening and I walked home in a state of exhilaration and ecstasy – on cloud nine. I could not get to sleep that night.

We had been members of the Orthodox Synagogue since arriving in Bradford. I had my Bar Mitzvah there and sister Winnie and Gerald were married there. My paternal grandfather who died in 1913 had arranged for a Sefer Torah (Scroll of the Five Books of Moses) special written for my father's Bar Mitzvah in 1903 for him to read (chant) from. Most fortunately we were able to bring all our possessions, including furniture, with us when we emigrated in 1937 and the prized possession – the Torah. I now read from this Torah. Subsequently both of our sons Anthony and Jonathan read from the same Torah. However, in 2010 I donated it to the Jewish Museum in Berlin. Whilst I was in the army my parents decided to join the Reform Synagogue. I was expected to follow suit but was not happy about it. *Rosh Hashana*, the Jewish New Year, was upon us when we would, as always, walk to the Synagogue. They were going to the Reform, but I said I would still go to the Orthodox. They said the family should stick together and that I should therefore go with them to the Reform, but I was still reluctant. All the way from home to the Synagogues, which were on either side of the main road only a few hundred meters apart, I was debating in my mind what decision to reach. I knew that by the time we reached the first of the two Synagogues I had to have made up my mind. I was in a real dilemma not to say turmoil. The site of decision came ever nearer. I had to decide at that point. I hesitated right up to the last second and in the end decided to join my parents much to their relief and pleasure. One of the elders Merton Arensberg who had not knowingly met me before asked me, in effect told me, to become burial secretary. As I was pretty green although I was 27 but wanted to make a good impression I assented, little knowing what to do in the event of a death. Merton showed me the ropes and I soon became proficient. Came the day when the rabbi who had been retained for a funeral could not attend and I was forced into taking the funeral myself. I was told afterwards that it had been a fine funeral. We then had resident rabbis who officiated but the last one left because we could no longer afford him, so I took funerals routinely. Rabbi Dr. Douglas Charing, who came from Leeds to take services was, certainly at the beginning of his tenure, a stranger and families preferred me as someone whom they knew. This produced the strange situation when I would ask the rabbi to deputise for me when I was away.

Also whilst I was in the army away from home Michael Roan, who had been so helpful during our emigration situation, suggested to my parents that I might take over a dental practice next to a textile mill which he owned in Heckmondwike, a small but lively market town between Huddersfield and Dewsbury. He had bought up a terrace of houses including this practice from which the dentist had already retired. In my father's practice, in which they had already installed a complete surgery ready for my use, it would have been difficult suddenly to support two practitioners instead of one. I therefor consented to give this a try without incurring any expenses. I divided my time 50/50 between the two practices. After a year I found that the Heckmondwike one prospered and I started paying Michael rent, eventually buying the property. Also, in the end I found that dividing my time was unproductive and as my father was on the point of retiring, we sold the practice to a third-party, Tom Muirhead, from Scotland who later specialised in implants, so I worked only in Heckmondwike. A fringe benefit there was that one of my nurses, Linda Barry, introduced me to computers using one of the first – a Spectrum Amstrad. Well done, Linda.

I had been appointed official registrar for weddings and, like for funerals, attended all the weddings in this capacity. I would also sing appropriate songs and thus became familiar with wedding procedures, so much so that I was invited to perform one or two weddings myself. Two of these took place outdoors, one in Hull, the other in Halifax. The son of my Berlin friend Hans in Hamburg, Germany, Alex had got married to his second wife Sandra in a civil marriage in the USA and now wanted a Jewish wedding in their hometown. As his mother was not Jewish no orthodox rabbi would marry them and neither of the two Reform rabbis were available. I got to know about the situation and offered my services which were accepted. So, we travelled to Hamburg and I performed the ceremony, in German, English and Hebrew, including singing appropriate songs and giving a sermon.

About the same time that we met the Franks (around 1955), we met by chance one of the boys from my class at the Jewish school in Berlin – Rolf Burchhardt, who had seen our engagement announcement in the 'Jewish Chronicle'. He had escaped to London, had got engaged at nearly the same time as us, then married Myra and subsequently had two boys Selwyn and Charles, keeping in time with one another, only we continued to have two girls. They came to live in Sheffield, so we saw a lot of each other. He developed colloidal graphite to lubricate heavy machinery and relates this story that he once travelled to the Continent by boat from Harwich to Rotterdam having booked an outside cabin. He thought the engine was very quiet – the shipping company was a client of his and he was pleased that his product was working well. He was less pleased when he looked out of the window the next morning to realise that the boat was still in Harwich. On enquiry he was told that the engine had malfunctioned and they had tried to telephone him but there was no reply.

The Synagogue employed a lady, Mrs. Plowman, who sang some of the prayers, but she had an operation on her vocal cords and eventually she could no longer sing. A member, Dr. Martin Kuttner, who was an anaesthetist in Keighley, had sung in a Synagogue choir in Berlin and with much work and determination found choral music, helped by my mother in transcribing and duplicating some of it, formed a choir of about 12 people who had never sung in a choir or anywhere before. With weekly rehearsals it flourished and soon I was invited to sing some solos. I found, however, that the quality of my singing was not good and fortunately sought singing lessons from another member Rita Morris, who was a professional singer. She put me through the hard paces which a beginner of singing must endure to make progress. After a year or more I thought I was good enough to join a choral society. The one in Bradford rehearsed on a Friday evening which was sacrosanct for Jews, so I applied to the Leeds Philharmonic for whom, as for any choral society, I had to pass a voice test. I ventured to take this although I had vowed never to take another examination after passing my university finals. Appropriately very nervous I presented myself for the slaughter, especially not knowing what I was supposed to sing, but passed with flying colours. I have now been in the choir for almost 50 years with a break of 3 years when Marianne was very ill and have just passed my re-audition. I have taken part in all the major choral works including performances in the Royal Albert Hall in London and other venues including Edinburgh, Birmingham and Tallinn, Estonia. I learnt the basic history of Jesus by singing in Bach's 'St. Matthew Passion'. In the meantime, Dr. Kuttner handed over the (Synagogue's) conductor's baton to me and over the years unfortunately one choir member after another disappeared and now I 'am' the choir singing everything solo. Our organist had been organist at the Cathedral and has a fantastic technique. The organist before him was a Miriam Clayton who was engaged to be married but her fiancée was killed in the First World War. She got engaged again some years later and again her fiancée was killed in the Second World War. She had a frail sister Nellie. When Nellie died and her coffin was carried out of the flat where the two had lived together for many years Miriam played Nellie's favourite tune on the piano.

Holding the Sefer Torah *especially written for my father's* bar mitzvah
in 1903. My sons and I read from it for our bar mitzvahs.
It is now in the Jewish Museum, Berlin

NEAR MISSES

I escaped death a few times in my life and relate a few incidents. I was told on just one occasion that my mother had a miscarriage before I was born, so the first narrow escape was that I might have been a miscarriage. The second was still in Berlin when there was a good snowfall and on my own, I took my sledge to the woods in Grunewald after which the district of Berlin where we lived was named. I was about six and enjoyed sledging down a mild slope and trundling up again to repeat. When it was going home time, I was tired and decided to lie down on the sledge for a brief rest. I am told that if I had fallen sleep, which I nearly did, I could have frozen to death. We were at the seaside on holiday, probably on the Baltic Sea. There were moles jutting out to sea to help break the waves as they came rolling in. These were wooden stakes in rows about two metres apart with the spaces in between filled with large rocks. My parents had gone for a swim but had left me behin. I decided to join them in the water, but they were on the far side of one of these moles. I entered the water and wanted to go round the end of the mole but found the water suddenly deeper than I thought and made for the mole for security. This was a big mistake because the waves, being stopped by the mole, created an eddy of water which gouged the sand away from the wooden stakes making the water even deeper and I was in imminent danger of drowning with waves crashing over my head. Most fortunately a man was near, saw my predicament and came to my rescue. He took hold of me and wrestled me on top of the mole. But the conditions there were as dangerous as before because they were coated with slippery seaweed, the large rocks were deliberately placed irregularly and waves kept breaking over the two of us. However, luck was on our side and the man managed literally to save me by clambering slowly over the rocks towards the beach.

We spent a holiday, probably in Arendsee (Germany). My parents or someone, had presented me with a large bright red aeroplane which I proudly carried around with me. On a walk we passed a herd of cows and presently the one nearest to us charged at the aeroplane. If it had not been tethered it would surely have gored me and the aeroplane. Even so the cow came at speed and the shock on the rope might easily have broken it. 'Jonathan's ship' was once moored at Zeebrugge, Belgium, a few years ago. Ships are tied to the dock with many very thick ropes, yet in a fierce wind that suddenly struck, these ropes snapped and the ship drifted away. Because it was so unexpected it was a while before she could be brought under control, re-docked and tied up. If it could happen to a securely tied up ship it could have happened to a perhaps too flimsy cow-rope.

About the same time, as I was sitting at my desk doing my homework, I was playing with a recently acquired present – a horseshoe-shaped magnet, picking up paper clip and such like. Next to me sticking out from the wall was an open-ended set of electrical orifices for insertion of a plug – a situation that was absolutely dangerous, yet ubiquitously generally in use at that time. I thought it would be fun to apply the magnet to the electrical points touching each of them with both ends of the magnet. Big mistake! There was a flash and loud bang and it is still a miracle that I survived 230 volts. My mother came rushing into the room asking what had happened and what the bang was. I said I had heard nothing. Nowadays electrical connections are made accident-proof and certainly designed differently.

Fast forward to Bradford Grammar School. During the war large buildings had to have a fire-watch team which had to be present so that if a fire broke out through enemy action appropriate remedies could be taken. Once a night a walk had to be taken to spaces that were not normally used during the day such as roofs to search for incendiary bombs, if any. It was pitch dark. Torches were not supplied and if they were had limited use as they could attract enemy aeroplanes. Two other pupils went ahead of me and I followed them. At one point they were some way in front. I was alone and had come to a T-junction, barely visible, and having to turn left or right. I chose left and eventually caught up with them. When I explored in daylight, I saw that if I had chosen right, I would have fallen many metres and not survived. In retrospect it was irresponsible of the other two not to have warned me.

At about this time on a hot summer's day I carried rubbish to the outside bin and found the ground swarming with live maggots. I got some methylated spirits, sprinkled it on the ground and lit it. It burst into flames immediately and had the desired effect of frying the offending maggots. When the flames threatened to die down, I poured some more spirit on the scene which could have ignited the flow of liquid right back to the bottle with disastrous results. That the bottle did not explode was a veritable miracle. But the maggots died.

Fast forward to when I was in the cadet corps at the University. We were on imaginary manoeuvres in the countryside when two of us were designated to carry out some task involving shovels. Having arrived at the site we decided to have a short rest. I actually lay down when presently my companion used his shovel to stick it forcibly into the ground only a few centimetres from my head. I thought he did it intentionally and considered that he could have killed me because there was no reason to stick the spade into the ground. I gave him the benefit of the doubt and merely said he should be more careful.

When I was stationed in Austria with the army our friends the Krips family came out and stayed quite near where I was billeted. I had acquired some sailing experience on the nearby Wörthersee and a small crowd of us hired a sailing boat which comfortably held the 10 or so people, the majority being children. None of the others had any sailing experience. The water was calm and a faint breeze was blowing, i.e. perfect sailing conditions. Life-vests in those days were not obligatory and were not supplied. We sailed out well enough but on the return trip a violent wind sprang up and tore at the sails. In trying to control them with fairly thin ropes, professionally called sheets, one snapped at a frayed part and the boat tilted to one side. I encouraged everybody to sit on the opposite side whilst I lowered the main sail to stop it from flapping. I was very frightened; the children thought it was all part of the fun; the adults shared my anguish. Eventually the sudden squall subsided and we paddled back to base, but only just.

Fast forward again to when I was about 60, I saw four drops of blood come out of my lower parts. My doctor properly referred me to a consultant who explored the inside under anaesthetic. I was not given pre-medical antibiotics to guard against infection 'because they did not want to wake me up to administer them'. Consequently, I got an infection, viz. septicaemia which could easily have proved fatal. I lodged a complaint against the hospital and had a full hearing, but they decided that my complaint was not upheld. Some months later I wondered if I had dreamed those drops of blood!

On my first visit to Israel I went to the resort at the southern end of the Dead Sea. From the rest area it was a hundred yards or so to a convenient place to enter the water. There was a small step down just before the shoreline and stepping down the clayey soil gave way and I fell backwards hitting my head hard on the ground. There were no untoward consequences but when similar events happened to two acquaintances of mine, they died two days after their fall from bleeding on the brain.

Driving home from Leeds after a concert in the dark in about 2017, I was about to pass a 'Keep Left' bollard when I saw a car's headlights coming towards me on his wrong side of the bollards. I took ultra-quick evasive action by going on the kerb and out of the way; fortunately, the driver behind me braked hard and disaster, if it had occurred, would have sent me straight to heaven. It was, however, averted by a hair's breadth and a split second.

God is truly benevolent and beneficent.

Settling Down

Still single I was introduced to a girl in London who, I think, had designs on me. I had given a talk in the Synagogue on a holiday trip I had undertaken at the end of my National Service to Yugoslavia, Greece and Turkey, which was reported in the national magazine of the Reform Movement. This girl wanted to see me again and invited me to repeat the talk to the B'nai B'rith group which met at the West London Synagogue near Marble Arch, which I duly did. At this talk there was a tall good-looking girl who caught my eye and who approached me afterwards to say that she too had been on one of these European express trains that I had mentioned. I was not quick enough to ask for her contact details and subsequently asked my sister Winnie to ascertain them from yet another girl who had a bit of an eye for me. I telephoned this Marianne offering to take her out for lunch a week hence after, I had spent a week in Scheveningen, Holland, for a dental congress and passed through London on the way back.. When I mentioned my name on the 'phone, she had already forgotten who I was. At the time she was going out with another boy but obviously not too seriously, for she asked her father, putting me on 'hold', if she should accept my invitation. He said nothing much could happen to her in the middle of the day and she should accept, which she did. The appointment was at the Lyons Corner House near Leicester

Square on Whit Monday – this was the only day which was convenient for me. I had my car in London and set off in good time to keep the appointment at 1 p.m. I chose the Inner Circle of Regent's Park and was most inconveniently held up behind a parade of dray horses by the Whitbread brewing company which I could not overtake. Mobile 'phones were not to be invented for another few years and I had visions of Marianne thinking she had been stood up and gone home. Pulling up where she was patiently standing and where it was forbidden to stop, I reached over to open the car door and said, 'Quick, jump in!' She had forgotten what I looked like but took a chance and did as requested. We had a good lunch, went to Windsor, then to a concert in the recently opened Royal Festival Hall ((1951) and parted, but I thought this is the girl for me. She and her parents came from Breslau, Germany (now Wroclaw, Poland), which was from a similar background to my family. Now how to keep up the friendship at 200 miles distance before motorways, when a trip by car would take up the best part of the day?

Marianne's father, Rudolf, also called Rudi, had been a judge in Breslau but lost his job under the Nazi regime. He was interned in Buchenwald concentration camp; fortunately for only six weeks during which time his wife Erna sought and eventually obtained entry visas to England where they became butler and housemaid to a solicitor's family in Timsbury near Bath and incidentally happened to live near the composer Sir Michael Tippett. They then moved to Bristol where they were treated very badly also by a solicitor and his wife and from where they had to leave as it became a 'Protected Area', i.e. vulnerable to espionage. Because a brother and family of Rudi already lived in Gloucester they moved there, staying temporarily with them whilst they sought accommodation, which they found in a small village called Kempley. There Erna worked in a cider factory and Rudi drove a furniture lorry and joined the Home Guard, a volunteer group of unpaid soldiers who would augment the army in case the war became more dangerous because of the possibility of a German invasion. There they were befriended by the local vicar who was very kind to them. Rudi looked to the future and studied accountancy – his knowledge of German law counted for nothing in England. He eventually passed the difficult examinations with high marks and secured a job at the United Restitution Office in London. They moved to Wembley Park just outside the geographical boundary of London. Marianne attended a grammar school nearby in Prince Henry Road where, by chance she was one of three Jewish girls in the class and with whom she became very friendly – Elizabeth and Joan. We saw Elizabeth who lived in London fairly often. She married late – a divorced man from her place of work but he unfortunately died whilst sitting on the upper deck of a bus having just delivered a lecture on pistols at the British War Museum. Sadly, Elizabeth succumbed to cancer some years later. Joan is married to a tax inspector Leon (retired); they live in Stockport. By sheer coincidence they own a timeshare apartment in Tenerife within a couple of hundred metres of our (now Deborah's and Ged's) timeshare villa and at the same time, so we can see each other there.

I saw Marianne only eight times in the next few months, but we corresponded and talked on the telephone many times. On one of her visits to Bradford I plucked up enough courage to propose to her on the train station a few minutes before her train departed – very romantic! We arranged to get married in the Liberal Synagogue in Belsize Square in

August 1955 with the resident Rabbi officiating. A few weeks before the day, everything having been discussed with him, my future father-in-law telephoned him to ascertain that everything had been prepared as discussed when he said casually that he was going on holiday including the wedding date. Hurriedly we asked the Bradford Reform Rabbi Dr. Erich Bienheim if he would come to London to perform the ceremony, which he did but at the big Liberal Synagogue in St. John's Wood. It turned out to be the hottest day of the year. We spent our honeymoon in Copenhagen. One day we used the short sea crossing to spend a day in Helsingør in Sweden and noticed that local people did not have to produce their passports, showing the way for the European Union many years later. We travelled to Copenhagen and back by surface transport, by through train from Hoek van Holland to Copenhagen and return by train to Ejsberg, then ferry to Newcastle. Flying was still in its infancy.

We had chosen to have a house built to our specification, but it would not be ready till May the next year during which time we lived in two attic rooms in my parents' house. Marianne was not completely happy about moving to Bradford having lived in London for half her life but with the help of new friends she soon settled down. We visited her parents a few times a year when we could also see her friends. Marianne sought a secretarial job and went for interview to A. & S. Henry, a wool merchant. Bearing in mind that our name was still Librowicz the interviewer asked her as she entered the room 'You do speak English?' Justifiably she was offended as she probably spoke a better English than he. Anyway, she worked there until she became pregnant. This precipitated two events: one was that I suggested that we spent our holidays in a place which had national health service (NHS) facilities in case she needed help in her pregnancy. We chose Guernsey as being a good holiday resort and though British it was 'abroad'. We flew from the mainland and landed on a grass runway with a wooden hut for terminal building – this was 1955. We found out later that, though Guernsey was 'British', the NHS did not function there but we had a good holiday. The other was that we had talked about changing our name to something less continental and now wanted the baby to be born with the new name. As Librowicz was a unique name I would have liked the new name also to be unique and eventually chose a novel spelling for Leavor. Her doctor had proscribed alcohol except in small quantities and on no account gin but as Marianne was a teetotaller by choice because she did not like alcoholic drinks, the advice was superfluous. I was present at the birth of a healthy Anthony. For the record Jonathan, then Deborah, then Caroline were born later. All have given and continue to give much pleasure, are a great source of pride and will no doubt be mentioned again.

About the year 2000 I met author Rachel Feldberg and composer Sam Paechter both of whom had ancestors who were German refugees. They collaborated in composing a chamber opera whose subject was the rise of national socialism and its effect on Jews in Germany. They enlisted my help in researching relevant stories of which they had scant knowledge which I was able to impart to them and which they incorporated into the libretto. One of these was the well-known fact that many Jews who had not only fought on the German side in the First Word War but had won decorations for bravery, etc., my father having been awarded the Iron Cross 2nd class and the Ehrenkreuz,(Cross of Honour). Even so none of these saved him from prosecution. Came the performance for which they 'borrowed' members of the (professional and very good) Opera Nort;, guests boarded a vintage train at Embsay, near Skipton, station and a steam locomotive pulled the short train to Bolton Abbey station. On arrival we entered the waiting room which was fitted out as a miniature theatre with a chamber orchestra in a corner. There was no scenery

Marianne

and singers sang from scores with a minimum of stage directions. The atmosphere was designed to emulate as far as was possible the train journeys in unspeakable conditions by Jews to concentration camps.

Marianne and I at our engagement, 1955

My children, circa 1976
Jonathan, Caroline and Anthony, with Deborah in the front.

DENTAL POLITICS

A particular patient of my father's had a full set of dentures made with which the patient was not entirely satisfied. Any dental procedure may need after-care and dentures are no exception. Any such after-care is always given freely and always without rancour. The exact details of the complaint are irrelevant. The patient, instead of coming back for a possibly simple rectification of any discomfort, complained to the relevant committee of the NHS. The official who received the complaint would usually invite the complainant to visit him in his office and where possible and appropriate to suggest that he/she visits the dentist again to enable him to put matters right. In this case the complainant did not take up this offer, assuming it was given, and pursued the complaint. In due course my father had to appear before the relevant committee and under the rules could take a 'friend' with him, which was myself. For various reasons my father did not acquit himself too well and coupled with a suspected antagonism against a foreign dentist the committee found against him and fined him a nominal sum. I was incensed and thought he had been unfairly treated but this may have been attributed in part to familial reasons. At any rate I decided I would try to get myself involved in dental politics precisely to try and prevent this happening to other dentists. I got myself elected to the Bradford Local Dental Committee (LDC) representing about 100 dentists and after re-organisation this was subsumed into the West Riding of Yorkshire LDC. Yorkshire, the largest county in England, which was in those days divided into three areas called Ridings: North, East and West, but for some obscure reason not South. By default, I now represented 1,100 dentists and eventually became its honorary secretary. I was then elected to the London based General Dental Services Committee which met about four times a year at the British Dental Association headquarters. This committee would be in direct contact with the Department of Health (DoH) and would have an input into the smooth running of the National (dental) Health Service. As a member of this committee I was occasionally invited to attend high-powered meetings at the DoH to discuss penalties for dentists who had been found in breach of contract (i.e. guilty) of major infringements, including fraud. The most severe penalty could be erasure of that dentist from the Dentists' Register which meant that he could no longer practice.

Quite by chance the chief dental officer at the DoH at the time was a dental surgeon whom I had met in the army.

TRAINS

In my early childhood I was presented with a fairly simple train set – a rather nice passenger coach and three goods wagons, straight and curved rails and two points – a right hand one, a left hand one and a clockwork engine. I would play endlessly with this, constructing complex layouts of tracks so far as they would allow it with the limited number of rails, always to be packed away at the end of the day to be reconstructed the next day. This inevitably ignited my great interest in railways, but it was not until we got married and had a house of our own that I asked Marianne if I could indulge in a little luxury and acquire a few railway artefacts. The 'in-thing' was a double O-gauge electric system in which the front-runner was Hornby. The minimum number of rails to satisfy my desires and the maximum which Marianne would (sensibly) allow was bought with four coaches and an engine to set up in one of the spare rooms, this time without the need to dismantle it at the end of the day. This gave me immense pleasure and inevitably over time I acquired more rails and coaches. When abroad on holiday I would buy more exotic stock not available in the UK. The layout grew and soon I had to involve a redundant table-tennis table to accommodate it and eventually was able to run three trains independently. Alas it is now packed up in boxes as the room(s) were needed for children's bedrooms.

On a short holiday in Bournemouth we came upon a local temporary exhibition of double O gauge Hornby trains arranged by the local Lions Club in aid of charities and organised by Messrs. Hornby father and son. I had joined the Bradford Lions Club, an international organisation similar to Rotary, where 70 or so people, one only from each trade or profession, met for lunch but devoted some of their spare time in organising events for charity. For a few years I was elected to be 'speaker-finder' for which I had to find speakers to address the club after lunch. The attraction of this Bournemouth exhibition for me was of course great; Marianne had no choice but to accompany me and we entered. I mentioned to them that I was a member of the Lions and we were promptly introduced to the Hornbys. The father was indeed the founder of the great firm and his son who had studied engineering, was equally enthusiastic. They had built a huge layout on which they could run eight trains simultaneously complete with electrically operated points and signals. We both were very impressed and I was over the moon. They asked me if I knew of a site large enough to display this exhibition permanently and I would have loved to have it if any of our rooms had been large enough. At the point of departure, they offered to sell me one of their surplus engines for virtually pocket money which I accepted. A fringe benefit was that father Hornby had scratched his initials on the underside.

Remembering the Holocaust 1

We had emigrated under control in 1937. However, in 1939 Marianne's parents were persecuted and emigrated with great difficulties. At the beginning of September that year, 1939, by chance my mother, sister and I spent a few days in Cleveleys near Blackpool with Gwen Clarke, wife of the geography master at Bradford Grammar School who gave me English lessons. Listening to the radio on 3rd September, which was a Sunday, we heard the Prime Minister Neville Chamberlain say that he had issued an ultimatum to hitler, who had invaded Poland, that he should withdraw his troops by 11 a.m., otherwise England would declare war on Germany. He would broadcast again at that time, which he did. A recording of what he said still exists at the BBC. He said that no assurance had been given and that therefore a state of war existed. Gwen burst into tears as well she might. It unleashed six years of atrocious fighting with millions of deaths including six million Jews and other categories of people who were in the first instance incarcerated in concentration camps and brutally murdered for no reason other than that they were Jews, etc. All this did not surface until after the cessation of hostilities when allied troops advancing into occupied territories and Germany discovered these camps, one of these Bergen-Belsen being described for the BBC by Richard Dimbleby. The BBC would not believe his report and wanted further corroboration before broadcasting it. Nine of my relatives and two of Marianne's, a grandmother and an uncle, perished so needlessly. The horror was so great that after the initial awareness of what happened and descriptions, discussions, research and memorial events and further references to what has become known as the Holocaust, such references to it were subdued. It was as if the excruciating horror could not be absorbed into people's consciousness and it was deliberately played down as being too horrible even to discuss. It was not till about 20 years later that the Holocaust became a topic for discussion and deeper research. Israel created an institution Yad Vashem in Jerusalem which became a Research Venue and Memorial Park for victims. On a visit much later going through the Children's Pavilion was particularly emotionally draining. On entering I was immediately plunged into darkness with tiny lights in a high ceiling shining like stars. A narrow path barely visible but outlined by small lights encouraged people to go along it whilst a voice recited the names of children, their ages and the town whence they came from one after the other. As one and a half million children perished the recitation would probably last several days, then to begin again. The path was about 100 meters long and progress was of necessity slow and when I emerged into daylight, I thanked God that I for one was alive and was spared those children's fate, but I was also completely devastated and disorientated.

Many towns in Germany and international towns constructed Memorial Boards with appropriate messages. Over the years more and more memorials were constructed and Germany has rebuilt many synagogues which were destroyed in the so-called Kristallnacht in November 1938.

Sir Nicholas Winton amongst others arranged

Kindertransport trains to ferry children to England, but only one child per family was allowed and no parents; 669 children were thus rescued. Harrowing scenes took place when trains departed, the parents hardly knowing where England was and fearing justifiably that they would not see their children again which in most cases was only too true. These trains set out from Prague and Vienna. The UK arranged for KIndertransport trains from Germany and Austria. Thus, many children arrived in England and where they did not have previously arranged addresses to go to, they were held in housing complexes in Dover. A cri de coeur went out to Jewish communities in the land to help accommodate children. A few ladies from Bradford went there and, as if in a cattle market, chose 24 boys to come to Bradford where a large house in Parkfield Road was quickly bought and a temporary warden installed. My parents' best Jewish friends were Marie and Herbert Eger. They had two children Kurt-Leo and Hannah-Ruth. We two children and their children grew up together being of similar age. Herbert had been a successful lawyer, but he would be unable to practice in England, so they delayed an attempt at emigration. Now my father recommended them to become wardens, which they fulfilled with distinction though it was not easy to supervise so many boys. Tragically one of the boys, Tergfeld, was killed riding a bicycle. Such an accident was distressing enough but especially so as the Egers stood 'in loco parentis' and the committee, headed by Oswald Stroud, had a double duty to protect the boys. There was great distress all round the community.

Winton had never talked about his part in the Kindertransport, but the BBC found out about it. In a TV programme hosted by Esther Rantzen many years after the war she arranged for Winton to be her guest and invited many of the original 'Kinder' to come as well. Neither Winton nor the guests knew of the presence of the other. Esther told of Winton's work of love then asked if there were any of the Kinder (now mature adults) present – would they stand up. About 50 people slowly stood up scattered amongst the audience. It was a magical moment.

The year 1976 saw a long and very hot summer, recollected many times in 2018 for similar conditions. I had the good fortune to have solar heating installed. Four glass panels were fixed to the south-facing roof through which water with anti-freeze (as in cars' cooling system) was conducted and fed through a closed coil into a copper cylinder fitted in the loft. Heat exchange takes place heating the water in the cylinder which would be fed into the gas boiler, thus preheating it before the gas boiler functioned, thus saving on gas. When the weather is very hot, water can be fed into the domestic system direct from the cylinder in the loft. This year (2018) I have not had the boiler on for two months or more.

In the 1990s a series of young women, some of whom were prostitutes, were murdered in and around Bradford. This went on for some years and the police pulled out all stops to apprehend the culprit. Marianne regularly played badminton with a few people and usually took the car to the gym. On this occasion I took her and she was going to ask one of the players to give her a lift home. She did and a friend offered to drop her at home, but she insisted that he drop her at the top of the road and she could walk the rest. These murders were in everyday conversation and the man had said the Yorkshire Ripper, as the murderer was called by now, might be lurking round the corner, but she shrugged it off with a laugh. She did not laugh when a short time later the culprit was caught and found to live round the corner from our house a couple of hundred yards away.

One of these victims was a particularly tragic case and 1 sent a letter of condolence to the parents (whom I did not know). At the inquest the coroner mentioned that 'a citizen of Bradford' had sent a moving letter and read it out in court (as was reported in the local newspaper) but without naming the writer. I wish I had kept a copy, but I hadn't and cannot remember now exactly what I had written.

The train lines entering Birkenau

Remembering the Holocaust 2

In about 1996 Heinz Skyte in Leeds founded a 'Holocaust Survivors Friendship Association' to whose inaugural meeting I was invited. However, by that time the Holocaust had become so well described that I did not want to become involved in more of the same. But the second meeting advertised a talk by a very good friend, Val Ginsburg, who had survived under dreadful circumstances in Lithuania and Dachau and I came along to support him. After his talk Professor Grizelda Pollock related her experiences and said, inter alia, that she was born in a camp. When she was about five years old, she asked her mother, 'Why don't Jewish children have grandparents?' This was a most profound remark which moved me greatly and converted me to join the association.

It has in the meantime become a centre for remembrance with testimonies, education, research and culture, and is known the world over. The association developed into education, where members would give talks to schools, etc. and as a depository of artefacts. For three years the Chairman, Lilian Black and four professional helpers Tracy, Emma, Nikki and Diane set up a Holocaust Learning Centre in part of Huddersfield University which is now part museum, learning centre and depository of artefacts., which opened in 2018. My small contribution is that I recorded the Hebrew mourning song/prayer '*el male rachamim*' preceded by Brahms' *Lullaby* which is played in the museum side-room when activated. I also sing this at Holocaust Memorial Events in the last week in January to commemorate the liberation of Auschwitz in Bradford, Leeds, Halifax, Huddersfield and Wakefield. One year I sang it at the national memorial event in Coventry's Belgrade Theatre.

Many German towns invited their expelled citizens back for a week's sojourn all expenses paid in order to make good the injustice done to them. Marianne and I thus spent a week in Berlin in 1978 and I say with pleasure that 'they pulled out all stops' to make the week a success. The Mayor Eberhardt Diepgen gave a welcome address, which brought tears to my eyes because he emphasised complete contrition for the obscene deeds of the Third Reich, as the Nazi era was called. The Berlin Senate publishes a magazine 'Aktuell' four times a year which is sent to all such people all over the world for them to keep in touch with their original hometown. I took the opportunity to visit the large Jewish cemetery Weissensee which lay in East Berlin in a 'foreign' country, viz. the Deutsches Demokratisches Reich, (DDR). In pre-war Berlin I had heard my parents sometimes say they were going to Weissensee for a friend's funeral and for some reason the name had a special mystical aura for me which in the event was deserved as many of my relatives, including ancestors whom I did not even know, were buried there. My pre-war friend Hans had worked on the cemetery during the war and in any case was familiar with going into the DDR. In his car we crossed at Checkpoint Charlie, the only crossing between West and East Berlin, without much trouble. I was astonished at the sheer size of the cemetery – roughly a rectangle with one kilometre sides. I was also astonished that it resembled a jungle. Trees, weeds and ivy had taken over every available space obliterating the graves.

The helpful office provided a plan and some names and numbers of graves of relatives, but we managed to find only one for logistical reasons, and that with difficulty, that of my great-aunt Cäzilie whom we called Ziechen, who had died shortly after our emigration. The reason for the wasteland was that the Jewish community who owned the cemetery, was small in number and just did not have the finances to keep the cemetery tidy. I decided to try and do something about it. Through a friend of Marianne's family I managed to get an appointment with the president Dr. Kirchner and secretary Dr. Hermann Simon of the East Berlin Jewish community and at a subsequent visit crossed over the infamous border by myself this time and on foot to meet these gentlemen to put my proposal to them, i.e. to create a world wide fund to obtain money from, in the first instance, relatives of those buried there and later by anyone who was interested. They were naturally in agreement but warned me that several people had intimated their intention to do just that and nothing had come of it. I told them that I was made of sterner stuff.

Back home I formed a small committee and opened a bank account. I wrote innumerable letters to Jewish communities worldwide seeking publicity, which I invariably obtained, and soon money began to come in. I then sought an appointment with the minister for religious affairs in the DDR through a local lady who had communist connections and who gave me an introduction to the DDR ambassador to London who happened to be visiting Bradford shortly. He gave me a letter of introduction to Herr Gysy in Berlin which also facilitated my crossing from West to East. By chance in the construction of dentures there was an instrument called the Gysy articulator and when in the fullness of time I met Herr Gysy I mentioned this connection and he was indeed a descendant of the articulatorman and the ice was broken. Subsequently I presented myself at the ministry and after fairly cursory security I met four ministry gentlemen with an interpreter who was dismissed when they realised that I spoke German. I told them of my plan with which they concurred. After all it was going to import foreign currency if nothing else. They then suggested that we paid a visit to the cemetery with which they were not familiar. In a ministry car we sped off, the driver missed his turn off and drove past. I was on the point of referring to the error but thought better of it. He then turned round and found the correct street.

On one of my visits to ascertain that the work was done as specified in the schedule and seek out the grave of a relative, I enlisted the help of one of the office workers, Frau Borgman, to locate a grave on the plan in a field which had not yet been cleaned up and which was thick with unwelcome greenery. We knew the row and number of the grave, but it was completely hidden from view. We hit on a plan that I would start walking forward along the row and she would start walking at right angles in the direction of the numbers. Our paths were like co-ordinates on a map and every half-minute or so we would call out to each other 'hello'. We were invisible to each other but could hear our voices. Eventually where we met was the sought-after grave. Over successive visits, sometimes lasting only a day, I succeeded in tracing the graves of all my ancestors, some of whom I did not even know or know about. Great-aunt Etta who committed suicide when Jews were rounded up for transportation, was buried there but had no stone because all the family had been taken away and there was no one left to do it. I arranged for a stone suitably engraved to be set. As my fund was a registered charity, I had to produce annual accounts kindly set up by my accountant without charge. I asked Hermann Simon for some information, but he had no idea what accounts were or what an accountant was. Presumably he was paid a salary and the state paid for what meagre services it provided for the cemetery. This was the communist system. The infamous Wall came down in 1989 and the Jewish community, now combined with the more affluent West Berlin Jewish community, took over the administration of the cemetery.

On the visit to Berlin arranged by the Senate I met Leonore Maier who was to become a curator at the new Jewish Museum. I arranged with her that we would come again to bring artefacts from my family to coincide with the official opening of the Museum. Having retired to bed for the night on the day before the visit the next day we watched TV for the news when pictures came through of what is now known as 9/11. The scenes from the US were unbelievable. An announcement said that all buildings, transport and 'everything' closed down, certainly in Germany (it was German TV) and probably in most parts of the world.

Many world leaders and people of importance and influence had been invited to the opening and some had prepared speeches suitable for the occasion but now hurriedly had to re-write them to take account of the new circumstances. Fortunately, I had the lady's telephone number; made contact the next day and she said she would open the Museum for us specially which she duly did. After I had presented my artefacts, we had a private tour of the Museum and thus became the first ever visitors. We also became very good friends with Leonore, who is now in effect deputy curator.

Later we met the chief curator – Aubrey Pomerance. He

instituted a series of seminars led by survivors of the Holocaust and in this connection, I have visited the Museum on average once a year to give seminars to students of varying ages.

REVISITING THE BALKANS

I had referred to a journey to the Balkans at the end of my army service in Austria 1953. I planned a trip to Yugoslavia, Greece and Turkey with the local regimental medical officer Gerry Church. On one of my trips to Vienna I had applied for a visa at the Turkish Embassy when I was approached in the waiting room by a man who out of the blue asked me, 'Sind Sie adlig?' (Are you ennobled?) I said no. He said, 'What a pity. Otherwise I would have invited you to a dinner/dance'. Gerry had not got his visa, so I set off alone and arranged to meet him at Belgrade railway station from the one through train a day as we had not booked a hotel. So I had to get up early every day to meet this train and eventually he arrived. Yugoslavia had only recently become normalised from having been an oppressive state and Belgrade still suffered from austerity. After a week we journeyed on a through train to Athens, passing Skopje which shortly afterwards suffered a severe earthquake, and which twinned with Bradford later. We passed Mount Olympus and made friends with a young Greek girl Nitza, who had been sent to Canada ostensibly to find a husband but failed. She offered to show us a bit of Athens and gave us her address. On arrival in Athens we were accosted by a tout who said he would pay for a taxi to take us to a reasonable hotel. As we had not booked anywhere, we took up his offer. It was reasonable but the taxi fare appeared on our invoice when we left. We visited the Corinth Canal and various tourist sites, including the Parthenon with which we were very impressed. We went to the opera to see 'La Bohème' in Greek and got talking to our neighbour who, he said, worked in the Ministry of Finance and who offered to take us round more sites like Lekavitos, the 'other' hill in town. We went to the ministry and without (in those days) any security checks were sent to his office where, we think, he was surprised to see us but asked his superior if he could take time out for us. He indeed showed us several sites. We enquired where Nitza's address was located. It turned out to be not far short of a shantytown. We found her house resembling a better shack and asked for her. She came and was unrecognisable. Where on the train she was smartly dressed now she appeared almost as a slum girl. She was obviously surprised to see us and when we reminded her of her offer, she said she had a headache.

We had booked a cabin on a steamer from Piraeus to Istanbul on SS Barletta – 24-hour journey on which we became friendly with a doctor in the Pakistani army, Shafiq Rehman, who lived in Rawalpindi. He seemed a pleasant fellow and we decided to share a room. We visited the obligatory Hagia Sofia, Blue Mosque and Grand Bazaar. On Friday evening I went to the synagogue a huge building finely decorated. Some years later it fell victim to a bomb attack, fortunately not seriously, but bad enough. Looking up train times for our return journey we found that the next available one did not run till a few days hence and we had to send a telegram to our army station to say that we were going to overstay our leave, usually looked at askance, but nothing was said on our return. Needing some more money, we went to an exchange bureau where the clerk offered us the official rate for our pounds, then came around the counter and unofficially offered us a much higher rate. Gerry and I booked on the train, which would take us as far as Salonika where we overnighted in a compartment of a train which stood forlornly and empty by a deserted platform, continuing next morning. Before the train left Istanbul, we walked up and down the platform and were approached by a man who carried a carpet that he had just bought. He asked us if we would take the carpet and get it through customs as if it were ours. We thankfully declined. At the border he was taken off the train by officials.

Back home I was asked to give a talk to the synagogue on my travels which I did. This talk was reviewed in the national Synagogue magazine. The review was seen by the girl in London whom I had met briefly earlier and who wanted to meet me again. This is the episode through which I met Marianne.

JEWS IN BRADFORD

There were two large influxes of Jews to Bradford: the first was for economic reason when many people, not only Jews, came for the wool trade. Bradford's water is very soft enabling wool, imported mainly from Australia and New Zealand but also locally, to be washed easily and Bradford became the wool centre of the world. Some Jews who had become wealthy founded the Reform Synagogue and obtained a rabbi in a peculiar way. West London Synagogue had engaged a rabbi from Hamburg, Germany, subject to interview. When he presented himself, they did not take kindly to his strong German guttural accent and advised him to go to Bradford where most of its members originated from Germany. His interview here probably took place in German. He was accepted and stayed in post for 49 years. His descendants right to his great-grandchildren have taken and still take an active part in the welfare of the synagogue. The second wave of incoming Jews took place during the Nazi era in Germany 1933-1945 when many refugees came. For the High Holiday services, we had to put chairs in the aisles as the benches were full. But with deaths and many people moving mainly to London membership decreased until the present day. In about 2012 a group called 'Friends of the Synagogue' was created who pay £5 monthly which helps to keep the synagogue financially viable. There is a loosely labelled group in London called ex-Bradfordian

Jews which meets every few years and has about 60 adherents.

At the same time that Jews arrived and for the same reason – wool – many Christian people came here and founded the German Evangelical Church in Great Horton Road. This thrived and was visited in the 1930s by that great theologian, Pastor Dietrich Bonhoeffer. Sadly, its membership, like that of the synagogue, declined, so much so that to keep the building viable for just occasional services the Delius Trust has taken a long-term lease on the building. Delius, world famous composer, was born in Bradford. Whilst a member of the Leeds Philharmonic Choir I have sung in his 'Mass of Life', a magnificent work with words by the secular philosopher Nietzsche rather than from the Bible as the title implies. In Berlin pre-war Bonhoeffer's sister, Ursula Schleicher, was a patient of my father's and when after the war the BBC broadcast a programme about Bonhoeffer my father got in touch with her and after she died carried on a correspondence with her daughter Renate Bethge and her husband Eberhardt. I met them a few times both where they lived near Bonn and in London when a bust of Bonhoeffer was placed in one of the niches outside Westminster Abbey. Eberhardt died at the beginning of the century and Renate is in a care home in Bremen. I am in regular touch with their son, also called Dietrich, who is deputy principal cellist in the renowned English Chamber Orchestra.

In about 1960 I succumbed to an urge to own my personal number plate on my car and was lucky enough to acquire ROL 4 which I have kept to this day. The 'O' referred to an ancestor whose name was Oscar. In anticipation of Marianne one day owning a car as well we acquired ML 501 which was kept in storage. In good time we bought a secondhand Jowett car for her that was manufactured in Bradford. The firm was privately owned and made medium quality cars, a step up from basic cars. Unfortunately, the firm could not compete with the large multinational manufacturers and had to close down. Deborah now has that number plate. LPG (liquefied petroleum gas) was introduced to the UK as an alternative fuel to petrol whose by-product of oil refinery this was. It was considerably cheaper than petrol, but it needed machinery and a bulky gas tank to be installed. I acquired this system and I ran on gas for several years being able to transfer the gas installation from one car to the next.

I had devoted much energy on keeping the synagogue going which was necessary because of low membership and therefore low finances. For both this work and the interfaith work I was presented by the Lord Mayor Bradford with a beautiful glass ornament suitably inscribed. Then I was nominated for a national honour by Richard Stroud, one of the first rabbi's great-grandchildren which resulted in my being awarded the British Empire Medal by the personal representative of the Queen the Lord Lieutenant of West Yorkshire Dame Ingrid Roscoe in December 2017 in the synagogue, Dame Ingrid coming specially to do this, a rare honour. Usually recipients of awards have to go to her office.

Richard also nominated me to receive a national award for 'achievers' over the age of 70 sponsored jointly by the Sir Sigmund Sternberg Foundation and 'The Times' newspaper. For this award I was one of five 'runners-up' for which the award took place in June 2018 at 11 Downing Street, London, the official residence of the Chancellor of the Exchequer. Earlier in 2017 I was awarded the annual Hans Renold award by the Heaton Township Association, Heaton being the district of Bradford in which I live.

Marianne's father, who smoked quite a lot, developed a blockage of blood vessels in his leg. Whilst his consultant was on holiday he had to be hospitalised and died with Erna and Marianne by his bedside, aged 77 in 1978. Erna reached the age of 90 ½ and died after a stroke in 1996 with Marianne, me, Jonathan and by chance Lucy, my daughter-in-law, and one-year-old James present. Precisely one minute after she died Caroline telephoned to ask how she was. I took both their funerals.

Erna and Rudi Bright, Marianne's parents circa 1960

Rudi outside No. 11 Downing Street, London having received a joint award from 'The Times' and 'Sir Sigmund Sternberg Foundation' for national achievers over the age of 70

MARIANNE'S HEALTH

In about 2007 Marianne could not shake off a persistent cough. Her doctor, having looked at an X-ray of her lungs, referred her to a consultant who diagnosed lung cancer although Marianne had never smoked. He recommended surgery. We said we had just booked a holiday in the Galapagos Islands, Ecuador. He said he had just been there and he would make arrangements speedily so that we would not miss out on going – he had enjoyed the trip so much. The operation was carried out by a surgeon with a very high reputation and who reported that the type of lung cancer was one which was specific to non-smokers. I enquired if she needed radiotherapy or chemotherapy after-care, but he said it was not necessary. The holiday was fantastic: none of the animals that we saw ran away when we humans approached. We especially liked the iguanas which looked like fierce prehistoric monsters. But the consultant, who was shortly afterwards promoted to a London hospital, was wrong because Marianne developed a secondary in the chest which, however, was successfully zapped by gamma rays which destroyed it. Sometime later when she did not feel well she had a swelling diagnosed in the brain for which the consultant again tried to zap it, but was not successful and put her on steroids. They did not work either. As she then kept falling, we had no alternative but to admit her to a care home where she survived for about a year. When she eventually died all four children, two of their spouses and myself were present at a very peaceful end. Marianne knew she was dying and was very brave in the face of it, never once complaining. The funeral hall was full to overflowing.

This Is My Funeral Oration for Marianne
(with some repetitions from elsewhere in this narrative)

There are thousands of stories in the Jewish and Hebrew literature. One such describes the death of Akiba. When they led Akiba to the executioner it was time for reciting the 'Shema', the morning prayer. With iron combs they scraped away his skin as he recited the 'Shema' acknowledging the presence of God. 'Even now?' his disciples asked. His reply was: 'All my life I have been troubled by the verse "Love the Lord thy God with all your heart and all your soul," which means even if He takes your life. I often wondered if I could always fulfill that obligation. And now I know I can.' During the last year or so of her life Marianne sometimes asked her professional carers and me how she would be able to tell when her sacred hour has arrived. What was going to happen? How will I know? Well now she knows.

Marianne and I have been married for 59 years but have obviously known each other for 60 and more years, so although God has not allowed us to celebrate our 60th wedding anniversary, we had reached the magic number 60 one way or another.

Marianne was an only child by design as Erma and Rudi Bright decided that after one child the political climate in Germany was not conducive to having a larger family and although they could not have foreseen the exact scenario of the difficult times that were to follow, comparatively fortunate as they were, her parents were right. As a consequence, Marianne would often tell me that she missed siblings and would invent one or two in her imagination, having dolls as substitutes for the real thing. The other consequence was that we decided to have a comparatively large family to compensate for the only child policy and incidentally to redress just a little the insane and obscene toll of six million Jews slaughtered during the Holocaust written about so eloquently by the historian Martin Gilbert who died recently. Marianne's father was a highly respected lawyer and judge but could not carry out his profession in this country and both parents carried out menial jobs just to survive mainly in the West Country, ending up for a while in a rural village called Kempley in the heart of Gloucestershire. One of the highlights there were the abundant wild daffodil fields which Marianne and friends were allowed to pick, bind into bundles of 12 and sell to middlemen for a shilling a bunch. Every year at that time Marianne would remind me of that episode and she was thrilled a year or two ago when 'The Times' devoted a whole page in its travel section to 'picking daffodils at Kempley'. We should all be pleased that we are today in the middle of a profusion of daffodils which helped to adorn her room. This gives me the opportunity of thanking carers in the 'Borrins Care Home' and 'Fairmount Nursing Home' and their managers who are here, for the exemplary care that they lavished on Marianne not only with devotion but also with love. Many doctors played their part in trying to heal Marianne. Dr. Hopkins of the Westcliffe Medical Centre actually prolonged her life by a year. Our grateful thanks to him and to them, more than I can adequately express. I also want to pay tribute, without any embarrassment to our children who pulled out all the stops to help during the last year and I want to pay special tribute to one family member who by chance was in our house when Marianne fell for the umpteenth time and I realised that I could not cope any more. I hurriedly booked a room at the Borrins Care Home, then had to tell Marianne that I would have to take her there. Though she realised the severity of the situation she turned a blind eye to it and refused to go. Even after much pleading and persuasion she employed delaying tactics one after the other. It was Ged who by utmost diplomacy, patience and gentle persuasion managed to coax her out of the bedroom where my patience was exhausted long before. Ged, you rose to the occasion magnificently and thank you a million for that.

Another highlight of Kempley was that their cat called Peter one day presented them with kittens. The low light of those times was when her father, together with thousands of other refugees, was interned on the Isle of Man as the then government thought that amongst all those refugees there could be German spies. How wrong they were!

We met as a result of a plan hatched by well-meaning people for me to meet someone else, but the plan misfired and by a series of coincidences we met at a talk I gave to the youth group in London of which Marianne was a member. A week later I telephoned for a date for lunch at the Coventry Street Lyons Corner House. She answered the phone and when I said who I was she did not have a clue – that was the impression I had made on her the week before. Anyway, she asked her father if she should accept the date and he said in the middle of the day nothing much could happen to her and she should go. In those days I still ventured to drive into London town, but along the Ring Road of Regent's Park I was held up by a Whitsunday

Parade of Whitbread dray horses and I was late. Eventually I drew up at the appointed place where I could see Marianne patiently waiting at the kerbside as arranged. I leant over to open the door and said, 'Quick, jump in' and Marianne did as she was asked hardly knowing whom she was going with. That, my friends, is how it all started. We hit it off immediately and have been hitting it off for a long time.

Born in Breslau, now called Wroclaw, she and her parents came to England in the nick of time. Incidentally, whereas they came from Wroclaw my father came from Inowroclaw, quite a coincidence and perhaps a good omen for our future. Anyway the good omen must have worked for we had a very happy life, enriched immeasurably by the arrival in the correct order of two boys and two girls and further enriched by the arrival by marriage of four lovely spice, er, spouses and even further enriched by the arrival in good order of no less than eight lovely grandchildren. Anthony even managed to marry a second time to an equally lovely lady. For a family tree I refer you to the programme. With a good professional life whilst Marianne concentrated on bringing up four children, where sometimes the older ones would help with tending to the younger, with the hobby of a strong interest in music on my part and with the wellbeing of the synagogue, life was very enjoyable. We were even luckier in that later our families lived very close to us.

Then the dark shadow of cancer came to test us. Luck ran out if I tell you that the lung cancer that Marianne had was a specific type for non-smokers. One wag suggested she start smoking to prevent a recurrence. But she didn't; neither did she drink alcoholic drinks, not because of conviction but simply because she didn't like any of them. We had to laugh when she went for her first examination at the doctors when she became pregnant for the first time when part of the advice he gave her was to avoid drinking gin. The surgeon who relieved her of part of her lung said she did not need any after-treatment, but he was wrong. Marianne survived two secondaries but developed a third. She knew the score each time but never complained. Her courage and stoicism in facing certain death was something I had not seen before in her and shows a strength of character which frankly I did not think Marianne had, but she did have it.

My friends, the question is often asked and with justification: why does God allow this to happen? I won't even mention the Holocaust again when God stood by to allow that obscene slaughter to happen. The late Rabbi Hugo Gryn said that God was there, crying, observing the carnage, but He could not do anything about it. And there are good people here today who have been involved with family tragedies. But Marianne was only 81 and looked forward to many years of watching grandchildren grow up and prosper which has now been denied to her. Through watching the older ones do just that and go to university she could project the younger ones going along the same path. Not that going to university is the one and only way forward. A good job is also an achievement.

Let me give you an analogy. It is often said that God works in mysterious ways which we don't understand. Imagine an insect crawling merrily on the ground. Someone comes along and even perhaps innocently lets fall a stone that kills the insect. In its moment of death, it thinks to itself, why do I have to die? What have I done wrong? It cannot possibly understand the sequence of events which has precipitated its demise. And, so it is with us humans. We cannot possibly understand God's ways with the world, however harsh they may appear. But there is one difference between animals and ourselves: we understand that we do not understand. To put it yet another way: we with our fancy calculators and complicated computers cannot compete with the devastating but so simple arithmetic of God, reckoning ages in single or double figures. Of course, all this theorising fails if you doubt the existence of God, but it still does not explain the tragedies which occur in life. You might have to find a different explanation.

We mourn Marianne's passing but let this occasion also be a celebration of her beautiful life, of her beautiful appearance, of her beautiful nature, of her strength in bringing up four children and going to London many times to tend to her sick parents. Once she came back in the evening and received a call in the morning to come to London again as her mother had had a stroke. She could always be relied on to rise to the occasion. Even though she certainly did not cherish the thought of dying she even managed to raise a faint smile an hour before she closed her eyes forever. That was the calibre of Marianne. I, the children, the grandchildren and you will remember her for a long time.

Dear God, you have guided Marianne's life while she has been here on earth though none of us may always have realised it. Now it is Your turn to look after her permanently. We pray that you will envelop her in Your goodness in a land over the rainbow, where there is no ill, no pain, only good health and perhaps an occasional touch of laughter. Dear God, take good care of her forever and a day, for this beautiful Marianne is very, very precious.

Marianne five weeks before she died. Anthony and Jane's wedding 2015

LIFE CONTINUES SOMEHOW...

Apart from the obvious complete change of mode of living and all sorts of circumstances which all bereaved persons will be familiar with, one double incident turned out to be a pleasant surprise. How can that be??? Both my neighbours are Muslim and would often visit and bring food round which has occurred even more frequently after Marianne's death. (As I write this it is nearing the end of Ramadan and I have several invitations to an Iftar, a meal eaten after fasting a whole day, mainly in Mosques.) But significantly both neighbours said earnestly that they hoped I would not move (into a smaller house) because they wanted me to be their neighbour and not be exposed to the possibility of being next to potentially unpleasant ones.

Many years earlier I had arranged a funeral when the rabbi whom I had engaged could not come so I had no alternative but to take the funeral myself which, by all accounts, I did well. Consequently, I have taken all funerals. I once took a funeral for a friend who was over 100 years old; she still had all her faculties and died in her sleep. She had lived in Memmingen, Germany where her best friend Erika still lived. She could not come to the funeral so I arranged with her beforehand that I would telephone her during the service using my mobile telephone, which I did. It was a magic moment much appreciated by the friend and to the amazement of those present.

STEPHEN SPIELBERG

One day about the beginning of the century the Synagogue's answer machine picked up a message seeking someone who was a refugee and wanted to go back to Germany. Ken Fabian asked me if I would respond. I contacted a lady whom I told that I was indeed a refugee but had no intention of returning to Germany except as a visitor. We arranged to meet at the ticket office of Wembley Park underground station some weeks hence when a smart young lady and I went to a local coffee bar. She explained that she and her film director friend were planning to make a film about returning refugees with reference to Berlin. I could not offer her a suitable scenario until a few months later when I received an invitation from my old Jewish school for a reunion of old pupils. This produced an immediate response and a film crew came to Bradford to film various pertinent aspects of my life and they were going to come to Berlin for the event, which they did, having obtained funding from TV Channel 4. They filmed scenes in the school, on the cemetery and in the theatre.

The American film director, Stephen Spielberg, was requested, after his very successful film 'Schindler's List', to research the subject further. He went ahead and founded an archive of survivors' stories, using in part the facilities of Universal Studios. He made a film and invited the subjects to come to Los Angeles for the première, all expenses paid.

True enough flight tickets arrived, and I spent a week as Spielberg's guest where I and the other seven survivors were extensively filmed again. We were treated like royalty and met Spielberg personally. The film was called 'The Lost Children of Berlin' of which I have several copies. The film was indeed shown on national TV.

Steven Spielberg (centre); Rudi and seven ex-Berlin school comrades from international places. Los Angeles, USA for premiere of film 'The Lost Children of Berlin' circa 1985.

CONTINENTAL DENTISTRY SOCIETY

A t the beginning of the 1940s there were so many refugee dental surgeons in England, mainly in London, that they decided to found their own organisation called Continental Dental Society (CDS) with a professor from Germany its President, Prof. Günter Türkheim. Fritz Salomon, who at one time was the secretary of the German Dental Association, became honorary secretary. The formation of this society was especially important because the British Dental Association (BDA) would not accept these dental surgeons to be members. They met twice a year in a London hotel for scientific lectures and demonstrations followed by a very fine dinner-dance..

My father was one of the first to join and when I became a dental surgeon, he took me with him to the next meeting in about 1953. I must have said or done something right for Salomon nominated me to be honorary secretary. I instigated a newsletter and introduced innovations, e.g. I had a scientific article translated into Esperanto which tried valiantly to be an international language. It was based on Spanish. However, it did not catch on and English has arguably become the international language. The CDS grew into an organisation with a very high scientific standing attracting dental surgeons of the highest calibre for lectures. Eventually the BDA accepted refugee dentists. As the older generation died out and more British dental surgeons joined, I suggested that the society change its name to Anglo-Continental Dental Society. After many years in post I retired from being secretary but soon afterwards the society decided to call it a day and closed down.

TENERIFE

In 1985 we saw an advertisement for a week's holiday in Tenerife for a very low-price including flights and bed and breakfast accommodation for one week in early January. To escape the cold, we took up the offer. Boarding the 'plane in Bradford in icy conditions we disembarked there in brilliant sunshine and hot weather. The accommodation and breakfast were pretty basic, but we coped. We spent one day hiring a car to circumvent the island and enjoyed the rest of the time by the adjacent swimming pool. The place was Los Gigantes, but we would have gone anywhere – we did not know the geography of Tenerife which we had, as long as we knew the name, idealised it as a paradise island. It was not far short of that description. At the end of the road it was a quiet and refined place overlooking the sea and a giant rock face, hence the name: The Giants. By the poolside we overheard other guests talking about the complex 'on the hill' but did not take much notice.

On the last but one day it began to rain a bit, so we decided to visit this complex. It turned out to be a quarter finished timeshare habitation beautifully laid out around an inviting swimming pool. The expression timeshare was explained and a show house villa was shown to us. We were given a list of prices depending on the time of year when a 'week' could be purchased. That week would then belong to

125

the person who could occupy it year after year. There was also an annual maintenance charge. We were given a taxi ride back to our basic flat and went for a meal. We were both so enchanted by this unexpected turn of events that we did not say a word till later on when the silence was broken and we could agree that we had seen a dream situation. Even the price was affordable and after a short discussion decided to invest in two weeks at the beginning of January (which happened to be the time when we were there) and the week before Christmas because it was really cheap – never ones for missing out on a bargain! The next day we went up again and signed up for Villa 48. This had a small kitchen with all appliances, renewed and supplemented over the years, a large lounge with French windows leading on to a large terrace overlooking the rock, a bedroom and bathroom/toilet, all furnished tastefully in Spanish style. It would be cleaned twice a week by maids with bedding, etc., changed once a week. A good restaurant was on site. Apart from being able to occupy those weeks as of right every year we could exchange the weeks for another resort within the company or abroad if we joined RCI, an international organisation which had access to a thousand or more such resorts worldwide which we did. We have now gone to Las Rosas, as the resort is called, for 34 years missing out only once and three times going to other resorts in the USA and Germany instead. The villa now belongs to Deborah and Ged (2016).

One of the added attractions of Las Rosas is that we meet the same people year after year who had all bought weeks for the same time as ourselves and they have become good friends albeit meeting them for only the same weeks in the year, sharing their fortunes and misfortunes.

Meanwhile back in Bradford we invariably got to know

all the other refugees and a few got together to meet regularly. We belonged to a mainly Austrian set – Krips, Wertheimer, Bayer who all came from Vienna and four Librowicz's, the 'outsiders' from Berlin and Breslau. We would meet in each other's houses once a month and for birthdays and New Year's Eve. In between there would be musical evenings: Maria Krips had had singing lessons and she and her husband Hans, who was a cousin of the conductor Josef Krips, and my mother sang songs by Schubert and anyone else, my father playing the piano. In between Richard Bayer would tell jokes, sometimes in strong Austrian dialect. Sometimes, if the party was only a handful, we would play Monopoly with great hilarity. Other refugees formed another circle called 'Kräntzchen' comprising Reiman, Ellinger and Layton.

A man from Leeds, Bernard Silver, addressed a Jewish meeting one day and suggested that we formed a B'nai B'rith group, a Jewish international organisation to whose Berlin lodge my parents had belonged when it was so abruptly closed down. There were so many joiners that two lodges were formed, a ladies' and a men's lodge. We would meet once a month with a cultural talk followed by a discussion and refreshments.

Our main charitable function was to visit Jewish people with learning disabilities in local mental homes. One such was a lady who had been placed in this home by her parents, of whom the father was a rabbi (who, she said, came from Russia), merely because she was blind, presumably from birth, at the age of 17. She was now in her eighties and although she had obviously led a sheltered life in all respects one could have a reasonably normal conversation with her. Another was a quite intelligent man who would usually be able to tell a good joke and was very musical, astounding me sometimes with his intricate knowledge. He just could not fit into society. We invited him once to join a small party of lodge members for dinner in a restaurant. When I asked him to choose a meal from the menu, he was unable to make a choice saying he would have what I chose. A third man had been a rabbinical student but had become mentally ill. He would always conduct a short service, beginning and ending with a sung payer with a short sermon in between, which he would write out on tissue toilet paper and which always made sense.

Though flourishing in their heydays one by one members left for one reason or another or died so that eventually the two lodges joined together but unfortunately it also had to close in time, but not before each of us four, Marianne, me and my parents, had been president for one year.

COMPOSITIONS

Apart from trying to play piano or violin I had often tried to play original tunes on the piano, sometimes with a colleague Arnold Morris whom I first met when we were both students. My first composition was a setting of a poem by Heinrich Heine: '*Du bist wie eine Blume*'. The second opportunity arose when both Anthony and Jonathan played clarinet in their Belle Vue school band and I thought I would compose a piece for them, but the impetus was missing. We were going on holiday to Milano Marittima, Italy and I took with me music manuscript paper. Sitting on a deckchair on the beach I started composing a piece for military band, which is a group which has not only brass but also woodwind instruments; but hardly knowing anything about transposing instruments such as horns so everything was written in treble or bass clef. I did not have the luxury of a piano to check harmonies and just ploughed on regardless anticipating checking these points when I got home. The piece was eventually finished and I called it '*Milano Marittima*' (what else?). After editing it at home came the laborious task of writing out the individual parts for the different instruments and submitting the whole bundle to the music master Mr. Hedley Teale. He accepted it and sometime later it came to its first performance which turned out also to be its last. Not disheartened I set out to write another piece for military band that I called *'Springtime'*. We had got to know Jürgen Scherf who was conductor of the police band in Dresden, Germany.. He gave me good advice and this too was finished. By this time both boys had left school long ago and Teale had unfortunately died. I had got to know Philip Wilby who was a lecturer in music at Leeds University and he was able to persuade a band in the USA not only to play but also record it. I now had three compositions.

We had met Jürgen in Piestany. This was (is) a spa in Slovakia which Marianne wanted to visit as she suffered from back pain. We went twice: the first time we flew to Vienna then by taxi just across the border. I was going to come along just as a hotel guest but changed my mind and opted for treatment as well. This was soon after the Wende, the turnaround when the Eastern states had only become 'free' a couple of years previously and conditions were still primitive by Western standards. However, the physiotherapy treatment was first class but the food monotonous. We went again a couple of years later, travelling by car. By this time Czechoslovakia had split into the Czech Republic and Slovakia. It was on this second visit that we met Jürgen and his wife Ingrid. I asked his advice on several points in my second composition. Later he became spokesman for the police in Dresden. We kept in touch and in 2017 I invited them to come to Bradford for 10 days and was able to show them the surrounding countryside.

Having sung in and conducted the synagogue choir for many years it occurred to me that as many of the songs we sang were eminently beautiful it was a pity that only those people who attended synagogue services would hear them. I therefore set about setting seven songs for soprano, chorus and orchestra but editing them with slight alterations, introducing repeats, altering (improving?) some harmonies, etc. I was then left with seven separate pieces so decided to link them with recitatives whose words by myself were based on brief references to the Holocaust, and purely orchestral interludes with an additional prologue and epilogue, making it into a performable concert piece called 'Enosh' (Man) after one of the pieces, a setting of part of Psalm 103. It was composed in the 1970s but not resurrected until about 2010. Our excellent organist, Alan Horsey, knew a local amateur choir who were able to rehearse the work and it was duly performed at the Holocaust Memorial Service in Bradford. Alan insisted that I conducted it. My niece Jackie Fleming's partner Kenny was able to record it on film. It has been performed three times since – once by the conductor of the Alyth Gardens Synagogue in London, Viv Bellos, who repeated it in the synagogue here. The local choir then repeated it at the next Holocaust Service in Leeds Town Hall but conducted by their conductor, Doreen Anderson. The soloist locally was Rowena Thornton whose parents both sang in the chorus of Opera North. With his permission I dedicated the piece to Alec Robertson, MBE with whom I had formed a good relationship, and whom Marianne and I visited in his idyllic house in Pulborough, Sussex soon after we were married, when he presented me with all four vocal scores of Wagner's 'Ring'. He was a well-known weekly broadcaster on music.

RELATIONS WITH PEOPLE OF
OTHER FAITHS IN BRADFORD

One evening about 2012 a Muslim gentleman called at the house unexpectedly to enlist my help in opposing an application by a restaurant to open near the Synagogue. His interest was that he was the son of the owner of a restaurant around the corner from the Synagogue. I agreed and was elected to represent both him and us at the appeal in City Hall. We won and this was the beginning of a close relationship with not only Dr. Zulfi Ali but also many other Muslims in Bradford. He directed me to the Carlisle Business Centre, basically a Muslim organisation, which donated £500 to the synagogue. Subsequently I was introduced to Mahmood Mohammed who was ward manager for Manningham, the district in which the Synagogue was situated. He had access to Bradford Council funds and was also able to award £500 for the specific purpose of hosting that year's Chanukah service, which he was able to do in successive years. He was a Muslim who was domiciled in Uganda, Africa and who was one of thousands who were expelled by Idi Amin many years ago. Through him I met several Muslims of high standing, in particular executives from the Council of Mosques. One has become a close friend – Zulfi Karim and his partner Saira who had a high position on Bradford Council. An iconic woollen mill called Drummonds near the Synagogue was owned previously by Jewish people but was now owned by a Muslim Khalid Pervaiz, who donated a large sum of money specifically to repair the roof of the synagogue which caused headlines locally and nationally. The mill was now used mainly as a storeroom and Khalid invited a few of us to inspect the vast now empty halls. There were 20 chairs standing in a corner doing nothing. I offered to buy them, but Khalid said I could have them free of charge. As we needed them in the Synagogue fairly soon and I could not transport them anyway and I was going away, I asked Zulfi if he could get them across the street to us. He assented; I gave him the keys and told him the alarm code. When I returned it had been done. Such is the relationship between Zulfi and myself that at a later function when parking was going to be a problem I asked him if visitors could park in the large car park at his nearby Mosque and if he could provide a shuttle service using his friends, which he did. He later said that as long as he was alive visitors to the Synagogue could continue to use the Mosque's car park.

I can mention with justifiable pride that the Synagogue had co-opted Jani Rashid, a Muslim, on to the council. This alerted the local, national and international headlines as a unique event. Drummonds mill burned down to the ground in 2016. At the Synagogue's Chanukah service at which before the advent of the National Health Service when all treatment suddenly became free, a collection for local hospitals took place, but after then a collection for the Lord Mayor's charity would be taken. It became a tradition to invite the Lord Mayor and the Bishop to this service. Whilst the Lord Mayor would change each year Bishops would be more permanent until they either retired or were promoted. One such became Archbishop of York. At any rate we got to know the Bishops in West Yorkshire very well so that interfaith relations with the Cathedrals and the Church was easily established. Latterly I would be invited to many Cathedral events, so much so that at a formal Synagogue function at which the Dean of Bradford Cathedral Jerry Lepine was present I remarked in my speech that [as Shabbat services only took place once a month] 'I seemed to spend more time in your Cathedral than in my Synagogue.' I have also got to know several local vicars very well. I have invited Christian and Muslim executives to preach sermons in the Synagogue at High Holiday services which they and we certainly appreciated. For Chanukah in addition to the Lord Mayor and Bishop Toby Howarth we have lately also invited the Hindu representative, Manoj Joshi, who had attended services many times, and the Sikh representative, Nirmal Singh. Thus, my association with members of three religions other than Jewish became known locally, nationally and internationally. Journalists came especially from London and Germany and two from New York, USA, arranged their trips to England to take in Bradford. Television took an interest and many private people have made contact. We have also made close contact with the Member of Parliament for my home and the Synagogue Naz Shah and the politician Baroness Sayeeda Warsi, both of whom are Muslims. Being now relatively famous I was invited to record a radio programme 'Desert Island Discs' on Bradford Radio. Baroness Margaret Eaton had been a Friend of the Synagogue for many years and a great supporter, as have the other two MP's for Bradford: Judith Cummins and Imran Hussein.

Holocaust Memorial Day 2019 in Bradford Cathedal. L. to r. Manoj Joshi (Hindu), Lord Lieutenant of Yorkshire Ed Anderson, Cllr. Susan Hinchciffe Leader of Bradford Metropolitan Council, Lord Mayor Cllr. Zafar Ali, Dean of the Cathedral the Very Revd. Jerry Lepine, Judge Laurence Saffer, Rudi, Bishop of Bradford the Very Revd. Toby Howarth

L. to rt. Manoj Joshi DL Leader of Hindus in Bradford; Nudrat Afza; Rudi; Zulfi Karim DL President Council of Mosques Bradford 2019

Jani Rashid, Naz Shah,MP, Susan Hinchcliffe (Leader of Bradford Metropolitan Council), Rudi. Inscription dedicated by Dr. Hans Librowicz, father of Rudi, many decades ago, but appropriate when the Synagogue was named 'Tree of Life' in memory of the attack on the 'Tree of Life' Synagogue in Pittsburgh, USA in 2018. "Etz chajim hi lamachasikim bo" "It is a Tree of Life for those who grasp it [the Torah]". c.2017

Naz Shah,MP, Rudi, Baroness Sayeeda Warsi. Charity Day c.2017

HOLIDAYS

Mainly for the benefit of the children, though we enjoyed the situations too, we often went to Italy. My first taste of Italy was when the Army had posted me to Trieste and I went on a day excursion to Venice. I was overwhelmed by its beauty, uniqueness and heritage. Later, whenever we were in the vicinity on one holiday or another, we made a point of visiting 'La Serenissima' again and again, walking along the narrow streets and coming on unexpected sights around every corner. Everywhere there were canals with gondolas being expertly manoeuvred round corners or obstacles by the gondoliers. Once venturing slightly off the tourist trail into the locals' territory I wanted to buy a can of drink in a local shop. A child served me and shouted to adults in the back room (in Italian), 'How much is can for tourists?' I spoke some Italian and understood what she had said but did not comment.

After the children left home and especially following my retirement, we ventured further afield. Our first long haul holiday was to Hong Kong. The flight path on the approach to the airport was very close to houses on both sides, so close that we could see washing hanging out of the windows. A few years later a new airport was built partly on stilts above water. As we entered the hotel bedroom the TV was 'on' and scenes were shown of the explosion at

Chernobyl which pinpoints the year as 1986. We explored a lot, wanted to enter a Mosque on Nathan Road but were refused entry because we were 'Christian', used the ferry across the harbour travelling first class for 'pennies' more than second class and took the very steep funicular to the Peak with a grand view of the whole area, including the stricken Cunard liner lying burnt out in the harbour. We took a tram to the terminus where there was an open-air market where many men carried cages in which were their pet birds. We used the newly built underground to visit the New Territories. Another holiday took us to China where, in Beijing, we had an excellent English-speaking guide, George. We took in Shanghai which pre-war was virtually the only territory which allowed free entry for refugees. In Bali we visited the monkey forest: an area about 200m square where monkeys roamed about freely and would come and sit on our shoulder, as in Gibraltar. Another trip was to the Galapagos Islands famous for not being commercialised. Animals would have no fear of humans and would allow us to approach them quite close. We were fascinated by the iguanas which looked like fierce dragons but were in fact not at all aggressive. Large birds would tolerate a close liaison. The Galapagos group consists of about seven volcanic islands. We lived on a small ship with about 40 passengers for a week. A 'plane belonging to an airline unfortunately called Ikarus had taken us from the capital of Ecuador, Quito, to one of the islands with an airport whence a bus took us a short distance to the landing stage where the wooden benches al fresco for embarking our ship, were occupied by seals and large multi-coloured crabs. Icarus, according to Greek legend, had wings made of wax with which he flew, unfortunately too high, when the sun melted his wings with predictable results.

Our love of animals suggested that we also made a safari trip to Kenya. After arriving in Nairobi, we joined four other tourists and a guide in a large jeep to tour in the Masai Mara game park. We saw at close quarters elephants, lions, cheetahs, hyenas, hippopotamuses, rhinoceroses, deer, impala, etc. At one point a cheetah was walking at a leisurely pace when the guide asked us to disembark from the jeep and to walk parallel to the cheetah which was then about 50m from us, but the guide took his rifle with him. The cheetah ignored us, but we were thrilled. Staying overnight in a lodge a flimsy fence divided the lodge grounds from an area where precisely at 6 p.m. about six crocodiles emerged from the close-by river and were fed meal leftovers by the staff. In another lodge monkeys would roam round the open-air restaurant and would pinch food from right in front of us. We stopped by a native village where we were told the transition from a youth to a man was decided if and when he had killed a lion which we thought went counter to perceived animal preservation. One night we drove through the jungle in pitch darkness with a searchlight sweeping the ground in front of us to detect if there were any aggressive animals hidden in the bush. It was an eerie experience, especially when we came upon about 10 hippos quietly grazing in a tight group by the side of the road. I daresay they were as surprised as we were.

At the end we spent a week in a hotel by the sea adjacent to which was a native village. A small derelict Mosque was just visible and we asked at Reception if we would be allowed to visit it but were told 'no, because we were Christians' as in Hong Kong. One evening there was an open-air gala dinner at which the locals from next door exhibited wooden carvings. One such was a magnificent elephant with which Marianne fell in love and I must admit it looked beautiful, but we had to wait till next day before we could venture next door to purchase it. We took the opportunity to enquire if we could visit the mosque to which there was no objection this time.

At the end of the tour the jeep returned to Nairobi, but we chose to fly, leaving our luggage in the jeep. The airfield was a grassed area with no attendants, the only building being a public toilet without doors. One small plane after another came and went and we had to ask the pilot of each one if it went to Nairobi. Eventually a 'plane landed and the pilot propped up the tail end with a wooden stick – a 'plane is designed to be stable in the air, not necessarily on the ground. He said his was the one. It was a six-seater and sitting in the front seats we could watch the pilot through the open cockpit door. I think there were fewer controls for him than in a fancy car.

We then flew to Cape Town, South Africa, where the grandson of the cleaning lady who used to clean for Marianne's parents in London, lived. He had made Marianne welcome a few years earlier when she jumped ship (Jonathan's 'Queen Elizabeth 2') and stayed with them a few days, then flying home. This time we stayed almost a week, taking in the obligatory Table Mountain. One day when Marianne went window shopping, I decided to visit the Synagogue. After two strict security posts I reached the payment cubicle at the entrance. The man wanted an exorbitant fee to which I objected whereupon he immediately offered a special discount 'today'. Having negotiated that hurdle I was met by a lady 'meeter and greeter'. She could not legally ask if I was Jewish but asked if I had been in a Synagogue before. I was able to tell her that I was chairman of my Synagogue in the UK. In the inevitable discussion that followed, it transpired that her grandfather came from Inowrazlaw in Poland where my father was born.

We decided on a South American tour starting in Lima, Peru including Cuzco from where we took a train to near Lake Titicaca on which we took a ride on a boat called Caroline, ending up in the capital of Bolivia, La Paz. This lies high up in mountains where the air is rarefied and lacks oxygen, so an extra-long runway is needed for 'planes requiring a long take-off run because their engines do not function as strongly as at lower altitudes.

After staying in Lima, we went to Cusco which has a magnificent cathedral. From there we took another train to Ollantaytambo halfway to Machu Picchu. Taking a walk there after dinner we came across a large open-sided tent by the side of the road exposed to all the detritus of passing traffic, in which were a couple with many children of different ages reclining on a rug with primitive disorderly furniture, primitive kitchen facilities, no privacy anywhere, the children probably sleeping where they fell, dotted around the floor. We hurried back to the hotel to fetch our camera having ascertained if we could photograph this scene from what looked to us like purgatory but was paradise for them. We surmised that this was nevertheless an exceptional scene.

We elected to stay in a small (and only) hotel by Machu Picchu overnight which was just as well as day visitors had to contend with thick mist over the area, but which had lifted by the next day. Not only did we thus have a grand view of the site, but it was virtually empty until the next group of visitors who would arrive in late morning, like us the previous day. It was a ruin of a city built many centuries ago but in parts in a good state of preservation.

The main thoroughfare in Buenos Aires, capital of Argentina, has eight lanes in each direction and when we crossed one car after another stopped to let us pass. Eating in an open-air restaurant we had been advised to order only one meal for the two of us and even that was too much for us to finish. The beef was delicious! The locals ate off wooden topped tables but the waiter before we had uttered a word honoured us with a paper tablecloth. Flying from there we stopped overnight in a little but charming town Mendoza, then went on to Santiago de Chile. Flying high over the Andes the 'plane suddenly lurched down and we both thought there was something wrong. It was only that having avoided the high mountains the 'plane had to descend rapidly to reach the capital at sea level in a short distance.

There we met Walter Borchheim who had been a pupil at my Jewish school in Berlin, but we did not know each other then. Emigrating before the war he had an entry visa for Brazil, but the port authorities would not let him enter the country and he had no option but to stay on the ship which went round the Cape of Good Hope and up the West coast of Chile where he disembarked at the first port of call, eventually becoming a long distance lorry driver. He married, moved to Santiago, had a daughter who during a minor operation was starved of oxygen and became a permanent bed-ridden invalid, but a very pleasant person.

In Sao Paulo, Brazil, we renewed our acquaintance with an ex-nurse of mine, Diane, who had earlier married a Brazilian, Clovis Suares-Suete, whom she met whilst on holiday in Switzerland. He was for a long time the leading dance-band leader in Brazil. She became an English teacher there inter alia teaching Brazilian pilots specialised expressions in English to use in an air emergency. They had five children, one of whom died of a brain tumour aged about 20. We also visited a lady of over 90, Edith Munter, who had been, with her husband, very good friends of my parents. Her first husband had been killed in his car when he was one of the first people in the 1930's to own one. He was trying to beat a train at a level crossing but failed. On the way back to the hotel we passed an embroidery shop in which Marianne surprisingly took only a passing interest, but I had spotted a particularly impressive pattern of a small town called Parati situated, we learnt later, on the coast halfway between Rio de Janeiro and Sao Paulo. I dragged Marianne into the shop and we conversed as best we could with the shop assistant who only spoke Portuguese. When we reached stalemate the owner, who had overheard the faltering conversation, came out from behind a screen to help in one of several languages that were mutually understandable. It turned out that his ancestors came from Inowrazlaw, like the lady in the Synagogue in Cape Town. The tour included a trip to Parati where we were put up in a small hotel that used to be the home of the last king of Brazil. It was a quaint and pretty little village which was the exit port for silver brought down from the mountains by mule to be shipped to Portugal, which made that country rich. It was very low lying and at high tide some streets were under water. At home Marianne embroidered the pattern acquired in Sao Paulo. Back in the capital we approached the Snake Museum where there was a sign in Portuguese stating, 'No Entry'. However, as we did not understand the language (!) we rang the bell and asked in English if we could visit. Surprisingly the answer was 'yes' and we had a detailed tour. Sadly, we learned a few years later that the building together with its artefacts had burned down completely.

By chance one of our South American tours coincided with the wedding of Paola, the daughter of Marianne's cousin Marion in Montevideo, Uruguay, to Javier. This was a lavish affair where the only drinks served were whiskey and Coca-Cola, neither of which we liked and with difficulty acquired some orangeade. Marion's partner's son was the Uruguayan Ambassador to Brazil. We had flown in from Buenos Aires and because this town and Montevideo had a duty-free zone arrangement due to their proximity; we as Britishers were waved through. Marion one day took us to her flat in a popular and fashionable holiday resort at the Southern tip of the country, Punta del Este.

Between Rio and Sao Paulo, we went to the Pantanal, a wetland region some way inland famous for wildlife, specifically caimans which are half size crocodiles. They would feed mainly at night, but the guide took us to a small beach on the river where they would congregate during the day digesting the fish they had caught earlier. Some were still hungry and would amble to a small weir where fish would be swept over from the higher lake. The caimans would lie open mouthed below and catch them as they tumbled over, an example of the highest gain for the least exertion. Having caught their prey they would move away and make room for one of their friends which had waited patiently for their turn.

In free time Marianne and I went to this beach unaccompanied to watch these beasts even closer and 'made friends' with one of them which stared at me open mouthed face-to-face. I had a banana and threw the skin into its mouth, but it merely lodged in its teeth, the caiman taking no notice, continuing to lie there open mouthed. I used a stick to try to dislodge the banana skin, then being close enough to stroke its head, but thought better of it. The guide

146

arranged a horse-ride, a 'first' for some of us – I had last ridden a horse in 1953. One of our group stroked his horse and whispered into its ear 'amigo!' (friend). Along the way we had to make a small detour to prevent the horses trampling on a caiman which was innocently sunning itself. He said, 'They do not like to be disturbed'.

We took in the Iguaçu Falls, one of the three highest falls in the world. By chance we could see them from our hotel window. We saw Niagara Falls on a visit to Toronto from the Canadian side and the Victoria Falls when we visited Zambia when we had to take a taxi to Zimbabwe and, as British people, had to pay an extortionate entry fee for a visa, but it was worth it.

A trip to India to see the Taj Mahal and wildlife started in Delhi. As we entered the hotel room with a wide-open window a large pigeon flew into the room: we thought we did not want to see wildlife so soon. We asked a taxi driver recommended by the hotel to take us to a typically deprived area and saw poverty and sacred cows at close hand. A bus-ride to Agra took us to the Taj Mahal, a magnificent building built by Shah Jahan as a memorial to his recently deceased wife Mumtaz Mahal in the years 1631-1653. In white marble embedded with jewels it defies description. I photographed Marianne sitting on the bench on which Princess Diana sat so forlornly just before the breakup of her marriage. It is justifiably an UNESCO Heritage site.

The guide took us to Udaipur, a small city with many lakes, in one of which a hotel was built on the lake bottom and in which we stayed. It was reached by a continuously to-and-fro small ferryboat. We wondered how they overcame rising damp when it was built several centuries ago. We visited Jaipur, a small city that only lasted 14 years before it was abandoned. It was approached by an elephant ride. On the way there we passed a man with a dancing bear, a practice now discouraged as it was cruel, but some people defy the law.

Back in Delhi a car was arranged to drive us to the foothills of the Himalayas. We were supposed to see a tiger and though the guide and our companions said they saw one in the foliage we were not persuaded. Later, on a walk through dense forest, we came across a group of about 25 children sitting in a circle with a teacher who taught them to recite the Koran by heart.

Over the years we visited China where we walked on the Great Wall, the only artificial structure visible from space. Its major city Shanghai was the only place before the war which accepted Jewish refugees without any let or hindrance. In Israel I visited Yad Vashem where the Children's Pavilion was most distressing. Iceland, where we saw its most famous geyser; Yellowstone in the USA where we also saw its famous geyser and a bear grazing peacefully 100 yards away from the road when the guide stopped the coach so that we could observe it; and Yosemite National Park where we wanted to see bears which were elusive, but driving along a road one of these suddenly crossed the road in front of the car. We exchanged two of our timeshare weeks for four in the USA, hiring a car and starting out in Pinetop, Arizona. From there we visited the Petrified Forest – a whole area of fossils and later the Painted Desert. We then drove on passing the Hoover Dam to Las Vegas where we spent part of the arrival day and one night, just as the guidebook recommended, taking in a show and visiting a casino where playing pontoon I won, then lost, so came out even. San Diego was next where we saw a magnificent aquatic display of seals and dolphins. Then north along the coast to Los Angeles where we visited both Knott's Berry

Farm and Disneyworld theme parks. The former was marginally better, but both were very good. In one of them I was ahead of the ladies – Marianne, Deborah and Caroline – and came across a booth a little to one side of the road with a puppet looking out of a Punch and Judy set. A child stood in front of it and had a conversation, by a hidden microphone and loudspeaker, with the puppet which seemed to know everything about the child. How was that possible? I soon discovered how the system worked. Just by the side of the road was a man, well hidden, with another microphone and speaker and having explored the situation, I quickly gave him lots of information about Deborah which he wrote down whilst I stayed with him. When my ladies had caught up with me, I took Deborah to the puppet which immediately welcomed her by name, hometown, age, etc., which I had (hurriedly) told the man. When written notes were exhausted, we carried on, me whispering information to the man who relayed it to the puppet's loudspeaker. It worked like clockwork for several minutes – all three ladies did not know how it was done and indeed it was very uncanny, until the information came naturally to an end and all was revealed. It was a superb trick.

Further trips were to Egypt where we saw the Sphinx and Pyramids, enjoyed a boat trip on the Nile; visited the magnificent stone temple façade at Petra, Jordan, where we rode on a donkey followed by a few days at Nuweiba on the coast in Egypt where Israelis could stay without having to show a passport if they came by boat on the Red Sea.

Jonathan, having reached the senior position of chief purser for the Cunard Line of ocean cruisers, had a large cabin and was able to invite family members to share his accommodation for free. We thus enjoyed many cruises to varied European destinations but including one or two trips across the Atlantic to New York. On a subsequent trip there by myself I visited the beautifully rebuilt site of '9/11'. Cities we visited included Prague, Strasbourg, St. Petersburg, Moscow, Paris, Riga, Amsterdam, Cape Town. In Marrakesh the highlight was a walk through the souk, an indoor market where hundreds of stalls sold anything and everything, including false teeth pre-owned (like pre-owned cars). In Edinburgh we saw a performance of 'Murder in the Cathedral' by T. S. Eliot. We had spent our honeymoon in Copenhagen but for our Silver Wedding we chose Norway and stayed in the little seaside resort of Balestrand and in the mountains at Vatnahalsen. In New Orleans we took a trip on a steamer called 'Naches' on the Mississippi River on which a lady played a steam organ: the sound was produced by steam being led through vertical glass pipes of varying lengths, the longer the pipe the lower the note as in a pipe organ, and vice versa. In Budapest we ate in a restaurant in which a gipsy band played in a corner. The band consisted of a few excellent musicians especially the lead violinist who superbly played at my request part of Sarasate's *Zigeunerweisen*, one of the most difficult pieces in the repertoire which is often used as a showpiece at audition or examination. One of the instruments was a cembalom, which I knew by sound from the *Hary Janos* suite by Zoltan Kodaly, but I had never seen one. In a break in the music I gingerly made my way towards the band. It turned out to be a cross between a piano and a xylophone whose strings are hit by a soft-headed drumstick and which sounds like – a cembalom. In Moscow, Buenos Aires and Hamburg we ended up in hotels which had a namesake in the same town – very awkward, but in the end solved. We rented a car to explore Andalusia in Spain including the beautiful city of Seville where by chance the annual festival was on. The ladies were dressed in their very best national costumes, as were the men, some of whom rode on decorated horses with dispensing sherry decanters and glasses as part of their costume. There were many stalls selling local artefacts and food. In Granada we visited the Alhambra, one of the world's most fantastic gardens and buildings. In Cordova we saw the Mosque inside which a Cathedral was built with innumerable pillars. There in the 14th century the three religions Muslim, Christian and Jewish, co-habited side-by-side and profited by each of its adherents associating with each other and learning from each other, making the region prosperous until Queen Isabella ordered the expulsion of Jews in 1492. On a river cruise on the river Rhône, France, we saw the famous half derelict bridge at Avignon, source of the song *'Sur le pont d'Avignon'* and passed the village Chateau Neuf du Pape, seat of the Pope in the Middle Ages and now the name of a famous wine. Wanting to spend a week in Venice instead of the many one-day visits we had done in the past we stayed in a hotel near the train station in Padua at a fraction of the cost of an hotel in Venice and took one of the frequent trains into Venice, but visited nearby towns as well. Vicenza was the birthplace of Andrea Palladio who lived in the 16th century, building magnificent edifices with grandiose façades; hence many large theatres are called Palladium.

At the Taj Mahal with Marianne, circa 1990

THE FAMILY

Anthony studied German and European studies at Nottingham University where he met Judi whom he eventually married; they have one son, Louis. Having worked for a stonemason firm he is now self-employed, having produced some very fine stone sculptures. After two false starts in employment, in one of which he won a prize for getting best results and went to Sorrento, Italy for a couple of days, Anthony worked for DePuys which make artificial human joints. Unfortunately, they divorced after 28 years but he is now married to Jane who brought two boys into the marriage. They found each other on the internet. However, all three are on good terms. They have a villa near the South coast of Spain. Jonathan studied hotel management at Bradford and Blackpool colleges, during which for a term he worked as a waiter at Claridges in London. He applied to Buckingham Palace for a job but they encouraged him to get his qualification first. But instead he applied to the cruise shipping line Cunard who employed him as a waiter. After three months they realised that he was officer material and promoted him to the lowest rank of officer from which he has worked his way up to Chief Purser. He has now worked for the company for 30 years on all three current ships, at present on the Queen Elizabeth. For a time, he worked on the iconic QE2 which is now languishing in Dubai harbour where after some years the ship has at last been converted into a floating hotel. He married Lucy whom he had got to know on his course, and they have three children: James who is a paramedic in Plymouth, where he studied; Rebecca who is studying art at Liverpool University and their third child, David, who studied IT and passed with distinction. Near the end of her second year Rebecca presented the family with an addition: Isabelle, making me a great-grandfather. Deborah studied nursery nursing and worked as such for a few years but they frequently sent her on 'supply work' and additionally many children only spoke Urdu, so she gave this up to work for the Council lollipopping [helping children cross the road] and as a dinner lady at lunch time in a local school. She married Gerard called Ged and they have two children: Daniel who has passed his three years' apprenticeship for motor mechanics and is employed by a motor mechanics firm; and Alex who was in her first year at Nantwich University studying dog management, but then terminated her studies, working now for Boots in Hebden Bridge. Caroline studied chemistry at Newcastle University and works in a senior position for a pharmaceutical firm in Skipton making drugs mainly for the veterinary profession. They have two children – Sophie and Oliver, both doing very well at Bingley Grammar School. Jonathan, Deborah and Caroline gained their certificates for the Duke of Edinburgh Gold Award Scheme. They had their awards presented in Buckingham Palace and by the Lord Mayor of Bradford.

Late news: Daniel and his friend Elouise have presented me with a great-grandson Arlo in Mach 2020.

When we were able to join Jonathan in his cabin on board ship, we have both been on many trips mainly to the Mediterranean, Scandinavia and the USA. Visiting St.

Thomas Island in the Caribbean I took the opportunity of going to the synagogue and found to my amazement sand on the floor as if from a beach. There were two explanations for this: 1) it was to remind people that the Children of Israel walked through the desert for 40 years from Egypt to Palestine or 2) to deaden the sound of footsteps of worshippers in Synagogues in Spain after 1492 when Jews were expelled or had to convert to Christianity. However, some stayed without converting and prayed secretly.

Jonathan and HM The Queen, 1990

Left to right: Jonathan, Caroline, Deborah and Anthony, 2015

Jane and Anthony signing wedding register 2015

Back row left to right, Daniel, James, Louis, David.
Front row left to right: Alex, Me, Oliver, Sophie and Rebecca circa 2013

Cunningham family: Ged, Deborah, Daniel holding Arlo, Alex. 2020

Great-grandaughter Isabelle

Jonathan's family
(Back row) Jonathan, Lucy, Isabelle, Rebecca, James,
(front row) David, Matthew (Matty) 2020.

The Brown Family: Caroline, Sophie,   *Grandson Louis St. John,*
Robert (Rob) [in front] Oliver. 2015   *his mother Judi Leavor*

Four generations: Rudi, Daniel with Arlo and Deborah

Four generations: Rudi, Isabelle, Rebecca and Jonathan

Gottardo family: Diana (niece), Claude, Yael Levey=Luisa (niece),
Jessica (niece), Winnie (sister)

Kenny Jenkins partner of Jacky Fleming (niece) c.2017

The whole family in 2017

Eloise, Daniel's partner with their son Arlo 2020

LOVE OF OPERA

My parents had always talked about opera and my earliest experience of such was with the 'Mikado' by Gilbert and Sullivan performed very well by local amateurs. They particularly mentioned Wagner's *'Die Meistersinger'* and d'Albert's *'Tiefland'*. Before the advent of opera companies in the provincial capitals and Leeds, Covent Garden and Sadler's Wells in London were the only venues for opera. When *'Die Meistersinger'* came into the repertoire at Covent Garden my parents encouraged me to travel to London and see it. This was about 1947 and booking in advance was virtually impossible. I duly presented myself at the box office and was told the performance was sold out, but I could wait for returns. After waiting a couple of hours in a draughty passage the man called me over to sell me a return ticket. I was hugely impressed by the performance and was hooked on opera. This was a good example of my parents' generosity over and above the norm expected of good parents. Earlier examples were that, still in Berlin, they presented me with a wonderful bicycle. In Bradford they sent me to a fee-paying school when free ones were available and that they made me a reasonably lavish Bar Mitzvah when money was still at a premium. Another example, again musical, occurred when I started collecting gramophone records. My birthday was coming up and I requested a set of two records and named one out of a choice of three, depending at the time in part on what was currently available but also bearing in mind the expense. To my very pleasant surprise they presented me with all three. Those were the days of 78 rpm (revolutions per minute) records which had a maximum playing time of 4 ½ minutes per side for a 12" record. In this context I can relate that for one of my father's birthdays all I could afford at that time of austerity was one record out of a set of three containing Variation 18 of Rachmaninoff's *'Variations on a Theme of Paganini'* played by Benno Moiseiwitsch.

In good time smaller opera companies like the Carl Rosa toured the country and I got to see many operas. Arguably the highlight of all operas is the 'Ring' cycle of four operas by Wagner and the whole Covent Garden Company came to Leeds to perform it. If I recall rightly, I could only afford to see one of them. Sometime in the 1980s I saw an advertisement by a travel agency for trips to Bayreuth, Germany to see the complete cycle inclusive of fares and hotel at a reasonable price. It was not Marianne's cup of tea, so I went by myself. Bayreuth is where King Ludwig II of Bavaria, admirer and friend of Wagner, constructed a purpose-built opera house for him. To see and hear Wagner there was the pinnacle of opera experience. There was a group of about 20 people who were all very knowledgeable and we had an excellent guide. Acclimatising ourselves for a day or so we were fired up with anticipation for the first opera *'Das Rheingold'*. It begins in complete darkness, even in the orchestra pit. As the lights were slowly dimmed and expectation was sky-high my neighbour whispered to me, 'This is it, then.' They were simple, yet magic words. The double basses started their pianissimo rumble and an adventure had begun. All four operas were magnificently performed on alternate evenings and when the last chord had died away a week later, I was on a high emotional plateau and walked all the way back to the hotel instead of joining the others on the coach. I did not want to dispel the moment of elation. When I returned to my hotel room after 'Die Walküre' earlier, I idly switched on the TV and quite by chance this opera was broadcast in full in a recording and I watched it again from beginning to the end, all 4 hours of it. I went to Bayreuth a second time a few years later when the production was nowhere near as good as before although the singing was again of a very high order.

The first conductor of opera at Covent Garden after the war was an Austrian, Karl Rankl. He brought the company to great heights from nothing as the opera house was closed during the war. I remember that the governors announced a competition for a new opera to be submitted under a pseudonym. This was won by Rankl but the opera house never performed it.

Some iconic scenes from operas come to mind: In Wagner's 'Das Rheingold' the giant Fafner kills his brother Fasolt. As he lies prostate on the ground with arms outstretched Fafner cuts off his brother's arm with a sword – a wonderful visual trick. In 'Götterdämmerung' Siegfried having been slain lies dead at the feet of Wotan and imperceptibly the ground with him disappears downwards. In Puccini's titular opera, Tosca tells her lover Cavaradossi that she has obtained a pardon from police chief Scarpia but that he has to go through a mock execution, the soldiers using blanks. But Scarpia had double-crossed Tosca and had told the soldiers to use live ammunition. When they fire, he naturally falls to the ground dead, but she thinks he is feigning death, as she had told him to do. When the soldiers have gone, she tells him that he can now get up. When he does not do so and she repeats her call to get up she sings, 'How well he does it!' In Puccini's *'Madama Butterfly'* Japanese Butterfly welcomes her American sailor supposedly her husband back after a few years' absence but not knowing that he had a wife at home all the time. As his ship approaches but still some way away she waves an American flag in welcome little knowing that he is bringing his wife with him. In Humperdinck's *'Hänsel and Gretel'* the witch, usually stereotyped as a small hunchback, with a long, hooked nose, black cloak and a wand, was portrayed in this particular production by Opera North as a glamorous, tall, fashionably dressed well-proportioned woman who seduces Gretel with poisoned chocolates. In Britten's *'Peter Grimes'* the mob, roused by anger against Peter with a view to killing him, is preceded by a man carrying a large cross as if to lend the murderous throng religious legitimacy. In Moscow we saw a stupendous performance of the ballet *'Romeo and Juliet'* with music by Prokofiev. In Rome we saw Verdi's 'Aida' performed in the open air in the Terme de Caracallas with the moon shining appropriately whilst in Wilderswil near Interlaken we saw *'Wilhelm Tell'* by Friedrich Schiller played out in the open air with a flock of sheep driven across the meadow stage as a preamble.

HÄNSEL & GRETEL

DANCE DUET from the OPERA

BY

E. HUMPERDINCK

New Dental Words
BY
R. O. LEAVOR, L.D.S.

PIANO & VOICE

Heaton Musical Publications,
76 Heaton Park Drive, Bradford BD9 5QE, United Kingdom

MUSIC TYPE BY KIND PERMISSION OF SCHOTT & CO. LTD

I used E. Humperdinck's music and re-wrote the lyrics to encourage children to brush their teeth

167

Tanz - Duett
aus Hänsel und Gretel.
„Brüderchen, komm tanz' mit mir."

New words by R. O. Lexton, © 1975.

Dance - Duet
from Hänsel and Gretel.
„Brother, come and dance with me."

E. Humperdinck

With your foot go tap, tap, tap, Round you go, up and down, 'til you are a
With your foot go tap, tap, tap, Round you go, up and down, 'til you are a

cir - cus clown. With your brush go up, up, up, With your foot go tap, tap, tap,
cir - cus clown. With your brush go up, up, up, With your foot go tap, tap, tap,

Round you go, up and down, 'til you are a clown. clown. Oh, you've done that ve - ry well,
Round you go, up and down, 'til you are a clown.

Fine

B R U S H you spell, Use your brush now ev' - ry day. Then your teeth will

thir - ty stay. With your brush go down, down, down, With your foot go

Da capo al fine

ITALY AND ITALIAN

In the late 1950s many of my patients were Italian girls who worked in the textile mills. Most could not speak English. At the same time, we tended to go to Italy for our holidays. I therefore enrolled in evening classes to learn Italian where I found that having learnt Latin and French these languages helped a lot and I soon became quite proficient, taking the O-level examination and passing it. So conversing with patients and on holiday was easy.

During holidays in Italy to benefit from good weather, sea and sandy beaches we usually spent a few days on the way back in a village above Merano in a small family run hotel Belle Vue. Conveniently right next door to it was a chair lift into the centre of Merano, so we took this mode of transport rather than taking the car. It was pleasant sitting in the chair watching the scenery and thinking of nothing in particular, a welcome relief from the usual hustle and bustle. Franz Klotzner, an Austrian from the original Süd-Tirol who was not best pleased when this area became Italian after the First World War, would choose German and Austrian guests (and us) in preference to Italians. He would trust his guests to help themselves to beer and homegrown fruit 'on tick'. What made Merano extra special was that my parents had spent their honeymoon there.

RETIREMENT

In the 1990s the government decreed that dental surgeons who were principals as opposed to employees or assistants had to retire at a certain age because they thought their practical skills would be diminished. The basic thinking was correct, BUT they set the retiring age too low albeit on a sliding scale initially until the system had worked its way through. My comment at the time was that if skills diminished for principals why did it not diminish for the other groups? Also, in the long run it caused a shortage of NHS dental surgeons from 2010 onwards. At any rate I had to sell my practice in 1993 but was able to continue working in my old practice, now belonging to someone else, as assistant but part-time. I eventually stopped working altogether two years later. The first thing I noticed being retired was that every day at home was the same as the next.

To celebrate my retirement from being a principal we went to America. I had located two boys from my school in Berlin, one near New York, the other near Los Angeles. Henry Gunby, né Heinz Günzburger, was in NY and Walter Bloch, né Wolfgang, was in LA. We stayed a few very pleasurable days with each and their wives Ilse and Sydelle respectively. Especially as flights inside the USA were discounted for visitors from abroad, we decided to go to Hawaii as well, first flying to San Francisco where 'planes flew every few minutes like a shuttle service, then on to Hawaii, actually Oahu Island. The inhabitants have a much shorter alphabet than our familiar 26 letters and use a different language apart from English. True to tourists' first trip there we stayed in a hotel near Waikiki Beach. The UK travel agent had booked us half of a penthouse suite at a normal price. Returning to the hotel one day we shared the lift with a group of Korean Airlines stewardesses, each one more beautiful than the other. They pressed buttons for their respective floors, then I pressed PH at which they all swooned. The beach of fine sand was on a little bay which was sheltered from waves. We saw a man with a metal detector going along. We asked him what he was looking for: he said jewellery. He obviously must have found it a lucrative exercise. One morning bathing was prohibited as a swarm of jellyfish had invaded the bay, but they had disappeared by the afternoon. Calling at McDonalds for lunch and being given change of a few cents the assistant picked it up as soon as she had put it on the counter and popped it into the staff box. Everybody in the USA gets tipped. We did a tourist trip round the island and the guide made it clear several times that he and the driver expect to be tipped.

Marianne suffered from backache and someone recommended a spa in Czechoslovakia called Piestany. We decided to give it a try. The original arrangement was that I would come along as an ordinary hotel guest but once there, as I had occasional backache too, I decided on the full treatment as well. Spa treatment in the UK then was virtually unknown. We had flown to Vienna from which we were collected by a surprisingly reasonably priced taxi. Once there and booked into hotel accommodation, part of the spa complex, we were thoroughly examined by the spa doctor who prescribed a routine of spa treatments based on local spring water rich in many different minerals, Marianne's being different to mine. Treatments would sometimes begin at 7 a.m. and finish at 2 p.m. We would occasionally meet in the room in between sessions and compare experiences. Treatments would be water based, physiotherapy, or mud baths where you would be lying naked on a special bed and covered from head to toe by hot specially cleansed mud for about 15 minutes. In the afternoon we would walk to the nearby picturesque town where, however, there was not much to buy except beautiful crystal or porcelain ware; even coffee and cake was simple, the country only recently having emerged from being behind the Iron Curtain, i.e. under a frugal regime.

Seats in four different dining rooms were allocated according to whether guests were Czech, Arab, Russian or other foreigners. Although there was a narrow choice of food it had to be ordered two days in advance.

The beneficial effect of the treatment, which we had booked for about 18 days, only showed its effect a few weeks later. We went again a few years later, travelling by car. By his time the country had split into the Czech Republic and Slovakia. One afternoon we drove to the nearest village, also a spa town, parked the car and took a walk in the local park. Before setting off for the way back we wanted to use the local facilities which naturally had two entrances each marked for men and women, but in Czech, so we did not know which was which. We waited to see which gender came out and when he/she did so we could not decide whether it was a man or a woman, so took 50-50 potluck and luckily chose correctly.

After he had retired my father developed a cancer behind his left eye which had to be removed. This was tragic enough but would have played havoc with his professional life if it had occurred whilst he was still practicing, as it would obviously have robbed him of bifocal sight. However, he was fitted with a prosthesis which looked very good. Unfortunately, he developed mild dementia over the last two years of his life, which made life for my mother difficult, but she managed very well and it is much to her credit. Only in the last few months did he need around the clock carer. He died peacefully at home in 1991 aged 90 ½.

My mother had a mild stroke in 1993 which necessitated hospitalisation. Whilst there, cancer of the stomach was diagnosed. As mentioned earlier her mother had died of this disease and it was the only malady which she was frightened of developing. However, though she knew she had symptoms neither we nor the doctors told her what the diagnosis was, so when she died peacefully a few weeks later with my sister, Winnie, myself and my niece Jackie by her bedside she never knew that she had the disease.

Sister Winnie and Rudi 2016

LOCAL POLITICS

In 2012 the MP for Bradford, Marsha Singh, died in office and a by-election was held at which a George Galloway, who had not had any connection with Bradford but stood for a party called Respect, was elected mainly because he promised Muslim women that he would emancipate them where they had perhaps had a life dominated by their husbands. He was voted in by a large majority. However, his promises were not fulfilled as could have been anticipated and at the next general election a local lady Naz Shah was elected with a moderate majority much to the annoyance of Galloway. Round about this time a conflagration broke out between Israel and Gaza which was most unfortunate from all perspectives. It had two repercussions in the UK that affected Jewry. The national cabinet was on the whole pro-Israel and Baroness Sayeeda Warsi, who came from a Pakistani heritage, resigned from it in protest as a matter of honour; and Galloway said that Bradford was going to be an Israeli-free zone. I immediately wrote to the Israeli Ambassador, Daniel Taub that, on the contrary, Bradford was an Israeli-friendly zone. By return I received a message that he would like to come to Bradford to address a meeting, which he did to a full house in the synagogue. Naz turned out to be very popular and when there was a snap general election in 2017, she was rewarded with a huge majority. Most unfortunately for her some journalists resurrected something derogatory she had said two years previously concerning Israel of which at the time no one had taken any notice. Now it hit the headlines and Naz was castigated, losing the Labour whip but was told that she could have it back a few months hence. However, she apologised in the House of Commons, which was broadcast, pleading ignorance and a degree of stupidity.

She had previously joined a so-called Faith Walk where a group of interested people would visit a Church, then the Synagogue, then a Mosque, which Naz joined before the storm broke. This was immediately after her first election. Then came the publication of her indiscretion and one of her first actions was to visit me as chairman of the Synagogue to apologise which I accepted as I knew her not to be an antisemite or anti-Israeli. Later she addressed a room full of Jewish people in Leeds who were basically hostile to begin with, but I think she won them over. She has since been invited to official Synagogue functions all of which she has attended, as have the other two MPs, Imran Hussain and Judith Cummins. Another Muslim who became a friend of the Synagogue and myself was Baroness Sayeeda Warsi. All this time I have also been on very close terms with the Executive of the Bradford Council of Mosques. In this context I want to say that I have been and still am in close contact with all Bishops in West Yorkshire, the Dean of the Cathedral and the previous Dean, now Dean of St. Paul's Cathedral in London.

I can relate this story: I was on a cruise on the Queen Elizabeth where Jonathan worked. I entered the dining room on the first day and was just about to join my assigned table at which eight guests were already sitting. Before I could introduce myself, before a word was spoken, my mobile telephone rang. I was a bit embarrassed, as I should have switched it off. It was Naz who shouted, 'Rudi, I've got the whip back!' I made a suitable comment, rang off and said to the others, 'That was my MP!' What an entrance and introduction! On a later cruise I shared the table with three guests from Cardiff. They lived adjacent to the orthodox Synagogue and were sometimes called upon to go inside and switch the lights on or off when it was forbidden for orthodox Jews to do so on the Sabbath or Festivals. These kinds of people well known in Jewish circles are called Shabbosgoys, goys referring to non-Jews. I had never met a Shabbosgoy but now I met three at once.

When Marianne was very ill the son of my Berlin friend Hans and his wife Sandra visited. I took them on a brief tour of the countryside passing the station of a privately-run short railway system, the Keighley and Worth Valley Railway, on which they promptly wanted to travel. It was a single-track line with a passing loop halfway along. Whilst our train waited on this track for the opposing train to pass the guide in our compartment pointed out a guide on the other train as being the UK Ambassador for Tristan da Cunha. All trains were slow so it was easy to identify people. Now dental surgeons know all about this South Pacific Island because it had been isolated for centuries with no chocolates or sweets being available, so the inhabitants had good teeth. As soon as ships began to call with sweets, etc., their teeth developed decay. Also, Jonathan on the QE had called there once so I had several reasons apart from my interest in trains to make contact with this man. Chris Bates modestly called himself The Queen's Representative for the Island.

HONOURS

The first recognition of my labour of love for Interfaith, Synagogue and Holocaust was at the instigation of the late Ruth Hardy who suggested to the then Lord Mayor Cllr. Michael Gibbons that I might receive some recognition. He promptly invited her, her son Peter and myself to tea in the Lord Mayor's rooms and before leaving presented me with a beautiful glass ornament inscribed with the insignia of Bradford. Then came the highest honour – my name appeared in H.M. The Queen's Birthday Honours List in June 2017. In addition, I was honoured by the Lord Lieutenant of West Yorkshire, Dame Ingrid Roscoe, who sent me a hand-written letter offering to come to me to present me with the British Empire Medal if I could not manage to come to her official residence. In the event the Synagogue invited her to come our *Chanukah* service in December to which we would invite important people anyway. Also, this way all my family could attend. The grandchildren and six-month-old great-granddaughter had pride of place on the Executive Bench the nearest to where Ingrid and I stood for the investiture, the older family members sitting very close as well. I felt extremely honoured but very sad that neither Marianne, my parents nor parents-in-law were present. In my short acceptance speech, I asked rhetorically what emphasis I could give to the word 'thank you'. I quoted Elijah who said that the word of God did not come in the roar of the waves nor of the wind nor in the earthquake, but in the still small voice. So it was quietly said but with emotion and devotion.

About the same time the local newspaper *'Telegraph and Argus'* in conjunction with the City of Bradford awarded me first prize – a large inscribed metal medal – as the year's achiever at a public ceremony held in a local hotel. In mid-2018 three events occurred within a month or so. Two invitations came to garden parties, the first at Buckingham Palace to which I took Caroline, the second at the Lord Lieutenant's official residence in Bramham to which I took Deborah and in between the presentation of the medal.

The Buckingham Palace day started well: Caroline, heard Chris Evans on his 'Wide Awake Breakfast Club' on BBC Radio2 mention her name and venue. Caroline collected me at 7 a.m., took us to the Interchange Station and we boarded the Grand Central through train to London. She provided breakfast with smoked salmon sandwiches and champagne which we consumed on the train. The only way Anthony could participate in the honour of the garden party was to stand on the platform of Pontefract station (he lives near Pontefract) where some of the Grand Central trains stop and briefly see us through a window. Alas, our train did not stop at Pontefract. Judi met us at Kings Cross and invited us to lunch in a restaurant in South Kensington. The sun, which had kept hidden now appeared. We three took a taxi to the palace and had a long photo session in front of the building. Judi then went home. We joined a long queue which, however, moved relatively fast. At the side gate we had to show the yellow admission ticket and two identity documents which were minutely inspected by police. We joined the throng of people crossing the forecourt into the palace, through a corridor and a room where photography was forbidden, a guide at every corner pointing the way, on to a huge stone balcony at the rear of the building with steps leading down to a meticulously kept grass expanse with a few tables and chairs. We eventually found a table with one vacant chair which I used whilst Caroline got some soft drinks in plastic cups. Caroline disappeared again to get two rectangular plates full of sandwiches including cucumber ones and pastries. The two couples who shared the table intermittently were a Jewish one from Southend and a doctor who liaised between Israeli and Palestinian doctors to treat people from both sides and was interested in my interfaith work, like his. Meeting both couples was a happy coincidence.

On entering the area as just described I kept saying to Caroline and myself – is this true, is it really happening? It was scarcely believable especially in view of my coming to the UK as a refugee not knowing what the next day would bring, good or bad? And now this. Marianne would have loved it.

Presently a group of Yeomen of the Guard in their red tunics carrying lances came down the steps followed on the balcony by Prince Charles, Camilla and Princess Anne walking very slowly but remaining on it whilst the National Anthem was played by a military band. They then came down the steps flanked by 'The People'. Amongst the entourage I spotted the Chief Rabbi but could not locate him later. Whilst I ate some of the goodies Caroline did a walk-about taking photographs of Prince Charles, Camilla, Princess Anne and Prince Michael of Kent. Near each of the Royals were tall gentlemen in morning suits and top hats who gently kept 'The People' in line and slightly back. Some guests had previously been advised that they would be presented to this or the other Royal as a special privilege; sadly not I.

Caroline on her solo walk met Dame Ingrid who had invested me with the BEM six months previously, introduced herself and took a selfie with her. She then came back to the table and ate her goodies.

Together we did some more walking about seeking out any Royal who happened to be in our vicinity, but they were thin on the ground having gone to the Royal tent for their tea. As it was now 5 p.m. with the party not finishing till 6 p.m., we sat on chairs acquired with difficulty in the shade of some trees and watched the very fashionable world go by. Ascot had nothing on this parade.

Near 6 o'clock Yeomen preceded the Royals departing and we decided that, as there was nothing more to see or eat, we would slowly make our way out. Almost outside, after going through another room again with a photography prohibition a man next to me said, 'Hello, Rudi'. No, it was not a Royal but someone who recognised me from functions where I had taken a prominent part. It was Robert Jackson, High Sheriff of West Yorkshire no less. At last there was someone who knew me though I did not recognise him straight away.

Some more photographs were taken from the roundabout in front of the Palace with the gilded figure on top of the Monument. Then a long walk through Green Park to a tube station on to Kings Cross and a long wait for our train back. Fairly exhausted we used a little-known waiting room with comfortable chairs, then boarded the train home.

It was a great shame that Marianne did not live to partake in this occasion in the same way that she would have loved to be a great-grandmother. For me it was an unexpected experience and very great honour, which I neither would nor could ever have dreamed about. All the work I have done has been a proverbial labour of love with no thought of reward. Many thanks go to Richard Stroud who engineered it all and who has himself been awarded a medal for achievement in another field.

The presentation of the Sir Sigmund Sternberg Foundation and 'The Times' award was going to take place at 11 Downing Street, London in March but deep snow prevented trains from running and it was postponed to 14 June. Richard and I had arranged to meet on the concourse of Kings Cross train station, he travelling from Leeds, I from Bradford. In the event his train was delayed by 45 minutes. For once the mobile 'phone really came into its own as he was able to call me from his train to mine to arrange that we meet at the venue. I took the underground to Westminster and walked along Whitehall past the Cenotaph to the heavily guarded entrance to Downing Street ready to present the invitation and passport for security. At 20 minutes before 2 p.m. when the event was going to start the policeman at the gate said I was too early but eventually he let me in, then through airport-like security search. I then ambled along Downing Street. Unfortunately the door to No. 10 was open so I could not photograph it, but No. 11 was closed. I rang the bell and a lady opened it; I said my name and she immediately repeated it and said, 'Come in'. For those friends who may not know Nos. 10 and 11 Downing Street are the seats of government of the Prime Minister and Chancellor of the Exchequer respectively and like entering Buckingham Palace a week earlier I felt even at this stage of merely entering a sense of high elation and honour. I was given a name badge, relieved of my mobile and holdall including my camera and ascended the thickly carpeted staircase, passing on the way the open connecting passageway to No. 10. Entering a large room, I was offered an alcoholic or soft drink and met at once Michael

Sternberg, QC, son of the late Sigmund, whom I was able to tell that I had met is father once or twice. Sigmund had been a very generous benefactor to the National Reform Synagogues Movement and its headquarters bears his name.

Presently the Managing Editor of 'The Times' Mr. Robert Hands and Baroness Rosalind Altmann, CBE entered. Michael introduced Baroness Altmann who presented the prizes consisting of an inscribed parchment and a cheque, reading out briefly what each winner had achieved. A professional photographer took pictures. Michael spoke again, then Robert. Guests then mingled till 4 pm. Coming away the door to No. 10 was closed and was photographed.

This was an unforgettable experience on the same level as the Buckingham Palace Garden Party. By coincidence I had visited the two seats of government within one week. Days to remember! But more was to come.

On 1 July Deborah and I attended a garden party hosted by Dame Roscoe at her official residence Bowcliffe Hall in Bramham. Though only a tiny village it was well signposted and an imposing gate pointed to the Hall. We were welcomed by DL Major Sam Hardy who left his post at the entrance to come into the car park to speak to us. He knew me from his three visits to the Synagogue. Alcoholic or soft drinks were offered on entering the large garden where 100 or more tables and chairs were arranged. Surprisingly I met many people whom I knew and some who knew me but for whom I was at a loss to know who they were. Items of food were offered by air force cadets. As it was Commonwealth Day musical and dance items were performed by different groups. Again, it was an imposing affair which we were very honoured to attend. Even the weather was kind. A presentation was made to Dame Ingrid as she was retiring from the position of Lord Lieutenant of West Yorkshire.

Richard also arranged for a 'Royal' to visit the Bradford Synagogue to reward me for my work keeping it going in view of the low number of members and for my work for Interfaith and for Richard's pride in having a sixth generation of his family associated with the synagogue. This took place on 14 March 2019 when Prince Edward visited the synagogue. He stayed for two hours and it was the only venue he visited in Bradford. This was my welcome speech:

Your Royal Highness, in welcoming you, Sir, to the Bradford Synagogue I am reminded of the well-known story from our scriptures. A man approached Rabbi Hillel to teach him the precepts of the Jewish religion whilst standing on one leg. Hillel did as requested and said, 'Do unto others as you would have others do to you. All the rest is commentary.' Whilst at my age I will not emulate Rabbi Hillel I am hard put to it to do justice to a right royal welcome in a few minutes.

On my right is a plaque commemorating the tenure of Rabbi Dr. Joseph Strauss who came to Bradford from Germany in the 19th century and stayed for 49 years. He ministered to German immigrants who came here to help build up the wool trade bringing with them technical know-how which the local population accepted with alacrity and together they made Bradford the world centre of this wool-trade through which Bradford became the 10th richest town in the country. They themselves became rich, built this beautiful and unique Synagogue but also financed many charitable organisations here and elsewhere. Please remember, Sir, the word unique.

Rabbi Strauss and his wife Alice, a Mancunian, had children of whom the eldest Oswald, OBE and his wife Claire had a son Roy, OBE who became a Deputy

Lieutenant. Both Ossie and Roy became in turn chairmen of the Magistrates Bench. Roy, husband of Reka, had three sons of whom the eldest is Richard who is here. There are thus four generations of one family closely associated with the Synagogue adding to our uniqueness.

That is not all. This Synagogue, though a tiny minority in what became a city at the beginning of the last century, proudly produced one Mayor and one Lord Mayor. In fact, Alderman Jacob Moser was the first Lord Mayor of Bradford in 1911. Two more people from the Jewish population, though members of the Orthodox Synagogue, became Lord Mayors. Though as I said we were a minority yet produced people in high office adding to its uniqueness.

Lately, the Jewish population having dwindled almost to extinction the synagogue has even so reached the fourth reason for being unique. By a series of absolute coincidences which could have made the plot of a novel, initiated by Dr. Zulfi Ali, sitting near you, the synagogue has established enormously close relationships with other religions under the rubric of Interfaith. We visit each other's houses of worship, so much so that on one occasion I was able to address the Dean of the Cathedral, the Very Reverend Jerry Lepine sitting just behind you, that I seem to spend more time in his Cathedral than in my Synagogue. The current President of the Bradford Council of Mosques is Zulfi Karim, himself having just become a Deputy Lieutenant, and we have become close friends. To guild the lily a few years ago we co-opted a Muslim, Jani Rashid, also present, to the Council, a welcome fact which made not only national headlines but became known world-wide. Not only that but in successive years we have invited high officials from the Christian and Muslim communities to give a sermon on one of the holiest festivals in the Jewish calendar. I must mention

Kahlid Pervaiz who has given a lot of money specifically for urgent roof repairs.

It is also unique, though I say it myself, in that my investiture of the British Empire Medal just over a year ago on this platform (we call it bimah) was conducted by the then Lord Lieutenant Dame Ingrid Roscoe who came here specially, a great honour indeed.

I suggest, Sir, that we are honoured that you have made the choice to visit this Synagogue, adding to the uniqueness of the occasion. In an idle moment I thought that the word unique in the dictionary should be followed by – quote 'as in Bradford Synagogue'. We also would like you to extend our best wishes and continued good health to your esteemed parents Her Majesty The Queen and His Royal Highness Prince Philip Dukee of Edinburgh. A final thought is to wish you a belated many happy returns of your birthday which fell on last Sunday. The Bible quotes Elijah when he said that God speaks not in the roar of the waves nor in the thunderstorm nor in the earthquake, but in a still small voice. Thus, I say a heartfelt: thank you, Sir. In the meantime, all I can add is: Sir, enjoy! And that is an order.

Meeting Prince Edward at Bradford Reform Synagogue, 2019

In front of Buckingham Palace in July 2017

Muslim Jani Rashid and Rudi.
Jani is a co-opted member of the Synagogue Council

Dame Ingrid Roscoe, DCVO, Ph.D., FSA, former Lieutenant for West
Yorkshire and Rudi at Bramham, N. Yorkshire, Garden Party 1 July 2018

EPILOGUE

Sad to relate four of our best friends lost one of their children, all academically highly gifted, to disease or accident when they had all their lives still to come to fruition. For parents to lose a child is the worst possible death scenario and we wept with them.

I am most fortunate in having reached the age, at the time of writing, of 92. I am extremely happy that all my children, their spouses (can the plural of spouse be spice?), eight grandchildren and Judi are well, settled, have jobs or are retired, as appropriate, or are studying and that the unexpected but very welcome great-grandchild is a 'Wunderkind', i.e. someone with an high IQ even at the age, currently, of one and a half. All have given Marianne and me so very much pleasure and honour. Though one should not tempt fate I am fairly healthy with the aid of some regular tablets, though walking uphill is not my favourite pastime. Not daunted by my age I have just volunteered to be an honorary chaplain to the three Bradford hospitals. This means visiting Jewish patients if they have a need to speak to someone. I don't think I would have acted any differently anywhere in my life. I hope I have made more correct decisions than wrong ones and not offended too many people, if any. Puck in 'A Midsummer Night's Dream' ends the play thus: 'If we shadows have offended, think but this, and all is mended.' I feel well; certainly, I feel much younger than my age and people tell me that I look younger. However, no one knows what the future holds. Many people die in their sleep in bed overnight and I give Caroline a telephone call every morning. Long may it continue.

ADDENDUM 1

Late in the writing of my memoirs the curator of the Jewish Museum in Belin Aubrey Pomerance unearthed an article culled from 'Der Israelit', the newspaper of Inowrazlaw the town where my paternal ancestors had lived, written on the occasion of my father's bar mitzvah in 1903. It is reproduced here in translation, the reproduction of the original (also a copy) is reproduced below.

Inowrazlaw, in Nov. As one of the most prominent and honourable, a wonder and perfection in our community, is Mr. Rudolf Librowicz, who is a model and an example for a realistic and true piety, ready and joyful for sacrifices in awe of G'd, and who encourages and fires up his congregation to awe of G'd and piety. An inspired Jew, an excellent *mohel*, a distinguished cantor, in deep devotion when leading prayers, [these attributes] do not deter him, even from his large store, which supplies the whole of Germany, from using every opportunity to uphold his joyous inspiration for Torah and good deeds. As in the ways and means in his house and in his store Shabbath is kept in holiness and presents him and his devotion to obligations as a Jew in honour and fills us with the pious wish of being fruitful and successful in Israel..

Last Shabbat Mr. Librowicz celebrated the *bar mitzvah* of his only son. For this occasion he ordered the writing of a *sefer* Torah with precious silverware and taught his son personally in the chanting of the Torah, so that the *bar mitzvah* recited the whole portion in the temple, chanted the *haftarah* in an excellent manner and filled the hearts of the listeners with true joy. Both grandparents who were present were equally impressed with the occasion and harvested today with joy what they possibly sowed in tears.

Rabbi Dr. Kohn bestowed on Mr. Librowicz, who devotes his spare time wholly to the Synagogue and to Torah, on this extraordinary Shabbat, the significant title of Morenu [our teacher] and if this honour is given to a Jew for Torah and devotion it is due in full measure for Mr. Rudolf Librowicz.

[There follows in the original report a résumé of the Rabbi's sermon] (A bar mitzvah is the initiation of boys at age 13 into Jewish adulthood. It can also mean the boy himself. – The store referred to is a shoe and boot shop. The title of 'morenu' is the highest accolade which a Jewish community can bestow on a member.)

When my composition 'Enosh' received its first performance with orchestra in May 2019 the programme was augmented by other compositions, one of which was Berlioz's 'Shepherds' Farewell' which I conducted. To make

196

setzt hin, welcher besagt, daß „auf Grund des ad 2
Nr. 1 aufgenommenen Vorbehalts im Falle des Be-
dürfnisses auch den Synagogengemeinden die Einrich-
tung und Benutzung eines eigenen Schlachthauses
werde gestattet werden können." Es ist kaum abzu-
sehen, wodurch ein besonderes Bedürfniß gerade für
Synagogengemeinden hervorgerufen werden könnte,
wenn nicht gerade dadurch, daß die Gemeinden sich
gegen die Anwendung des Schächtschnittes ablehnend
verhalten und diesem Standpunkte durch entsprechende
Vorschriften für den Betrieb in dem allgemeinen
Schlachthause Ausdruck geben könnten."
Das ist ein richtiger Standpunkt. Wo die Stadt
das Schlachthaus zum Schächten nicht hergibt, kann
sich jeder jüdische Metzger eine Schächtstätte errichten.
Die jüdischen Stadtbewohner müssen dann darauf an-
tragen, daß sie von dem Theil der Steuern, der für
das Schlachthaus nöthig ist, befreit werden.

Inowrazlaw, im Nov. Als eines der hervor-
ragendsten und verdienstvollsten ‏עובד צבור‏ in un-
serer Gemeinde gilt Herr Rudolf Librowicz, der
als Muster und Vorbild echter, wahrer Frömmigkeit,
opferwilliger und opferfreudiger Gottesfurcht auch
seine Nebenmenschen zur Gottesfurcht und Frömmigkeit anspornt und anfeuert. Ein begeisterter Jehudi,
ein vortrefflicher Mohel, ein ausgezeichneter Baal
Kore, ein von tiefer Andacht erfüllter Baal Tefilah,
läßt er sich von seinem großen Geschäft, das sich über
ganz Deutschland erstreckt, nicht abhalten, jede Gelegen-
heit zu benutzen, um seine glühende Liebe zum Juden-
thum, seine freudige Begeisterung für Thora und Miz-
woth praktisch zu bethätigen. Die Art und Weise, wie
in seinem Hause, in seinem Geschäfte der Sabbat ge-
heiligt und gehalten wird, gereicht ihm und seiner
Pflichttreue als Jehudi zur Ehre und erfüllt uns mit
dem frommen Wunsche ‏ירבו כמותך בישראל‏!
Am jüngsten Sabbat ‏שמות‏ feierte Herr Librowicz
die Bar Mizwah seines einzigen Sohnes. Zu diesem
Zwecke ließ er eine Sefer Thora schreiben, kostbares
‏כלי קדש‏ für das Sefer anfertigen, unterrichtete seinen
Sohn persönlich in ‏טעמי המקרא‏, so daß der Bar
Mizwah die ganze Sidra in vollendeter Weise im Tem-
pel vorgelesen, die Hafthora in ausgezeichneter Weise
vorgetragen und das Herz der Zuhörer mit wahrer
Freude erfüllte. Die beiden Großeltern, die anwesend
waren, sind von demselben Geiste der Jirah beseelt,
und ernteten heute mit Jubel, was sie einst vielleicht
mit Thränen gesät.
Der Rabbiner, Herr Dr. Kohn, verlieh Herrn
Librowicz, der seine ganze freie Zeit dem Beth-Hami-
drasch resp. der Thora widmet, an diesem bedeutungs-
vollen Sabbate den Titel „Morenu", und wenn einem
Jehudi für Thora, Abodah und Gemilath Chassodim
dieser Titel gebührt, so gebührt er in vollem und
reichem Maße Herrn Rudolf Librowicz.

Durch eine Predigt von Seiten des Rabbiners
wurde der ‏ברכת גומל‏ unter der Theilnahme eines
sehr zahlreichen Auditoriums vollzogen, über den In-
halt der Predigt, will ich nächstens s. G. und soweit es
die Treue meines Gedächtnisses zuläßt, einiges mit-
theilen.

Zweibrücken. Ein Prozeß, wie er wohl noch
selten vorgekommen, beschäftigt seit einiger Zeit unsere
Gerichte. Die hiesige israelitische Gemeinde, vertreten
durch Rechtsanwalt Justizrath Rosenberger, hat gegen
den Bezirksrabbiner Dr. E. Meyer beim hiesigen Land-
gericht die Klage auf Auflösung des Dienstvertrages
angestellt, weil nach der Behauptung der Gemeinde der
Bezirksrabbiner die ihm obliegenden dienstlichen Ver-
pflichtungen nicht erfüllt und auch andere nicht näher
angegebene Gründe für die Lösung des Vertragsverhält-
nisses vorliegen. Die Kultusgemeinde hatte sich zu-
nächst beschwerdeführend an die Regierung und an das
Kultusministerium gewandt, woraufhin die Regierung
dem Bezirksrabbiner ihre entschiedene Mißbilligung
kundgegeben und schließlich auch angedroht habe, daß
sie die Genehmigung zur eventuellen Dienstentlassung
nicht versagen werde. Dabei wurde aber von Seiten
der Verwaltungsbehörden zugleich entschieden, daß
das zwischen dem Bezirksrabbiner und den Kultus-
gemeinden bestehende Vertragsverhältniß rein zivil-
rechtlicher Natur sei und daß die Dienstentlassung nur
nach den zivilrechtlichen Normen erfolgen könne. Die
Kultusgemeinde hat darauf dem Rabbiner die Dienstentlassung erklärt und, da derselbe nicht hiermit ein-
verstanden war, Auflösungsklage beim Zivilgericht
erhoben. Schon in der Klageschrift hat sie für ihre
Aufstellungen einen umfangreichen Beweis angeboten.
Wie auch die Verhältnisse liegen mögen — es wäre
dringend zu wünschen, daß von beiden Seiten die
Hand zur friedlichen Einigung geboten würde.. Ein
solcher Streit gehört nicht vor die Gerichte.

Wilhelmshaven, im Nov. Seit Bestehen der
Gemeinde fand in diesem Jahre zum ersten Male die
Vorbereitung zur Eidesleistung der jüdischen Rekruten
in der hiesigen Synagoge statt. Die Rekruten wurden
von Vorgesetzten zum Gottesdienste geführt. Dem
Gottesdienste wohnten Vertreter der Behörde und die
ganze Gemeinde bei.
Das Schreiben der Marinebehörde, worin dem
Ersuchen zur Abhaltung des Gottesdienstes Folge ge-
leistet wird, hat folgenden Wortlaut:
Kommando d. R. B. etc.
Wilhelmshaven, 21. Okt. 1903.
Auf das gefällige Schreiben vom 14. d. Mts.
Die Beeidigung der Oktoberrekruten findet am
24. d. Mts. statt. Die Rekruten jüdischen Glaubens
1) von der zweiten Matrosendivision und 2) von der
Stammkompagnie des dritten Seebataillons werden
Anweisung erhalten, sich am 23. dss. Mts., Vormittags

up a shortfall in the tenor section of the choir the conductor Steve Muir asked some musicians he knew to make up the numbers. One of these was Martin Pickard who was on the staff of Opera North who occasionally conducted operas for the company and who for a couple of years was chorus master of the Leeds Philharmonic Choir with whom I sang for 50 years. This now was truly a situation of the 'Sorcerer's Apprentice'. It also enabled me to realise a life long dream to conduct a symphony orchestra. An additional accolade was that two singers asked me for my autograph.

ADDENDUM 2

There follow some anecdotes, some of which are true and some are just funny stories which I thought I might share with you.

Three true stories about Nina Lewis, née Israelstam and her husband Louis: Nina's' father was rabbi in Bradford for 42 years (1921-1962) who, inter alia, prepared me for my bar mitzvah. She married a paintbrush manufacturer who also occasionally painted, mainly flowers. One day in 2013, when she was 90-years young, Nina was planning to take the tube from Baker Street, one of the stations on the London Underground, whose platform was on a bend. There is a recurrent loudspeaker announcement each time a train enters – MIND THE GAP of which Nina was well aware. She started to board a train in the middle of the coach where the gap was the widest, had one foot in the coach when the doors suddenly and unexpectedly started to close. She reflexively recoiled, stepped backwards and plunged six feet down into the narrow gap between platform edge and train carriage – landing with a mighty jolt on the concrete bed beneath the train track. Instant action followed; she was lifted back on to the platform miraculously suffering no broken bones though she did sustain substantial bruising throughout her body – from which she eventually recovered. (Fortunately, the electric rail at stations is always on the opposite side of the platform).

On one occasion her husband Louis showed me an album of photographs of some of his paintings. My comment on one was that the flowers looked artificial whereupon he replied that what he had painted were artificial flowers!

When he was nearly 93, with his health failing, and not wanting to be a burden on his beloved Nina, he came up with a very gentle way to have a graceful, painless exit that didn't distress his family. Over a period of several weeks, he subtly adjusted the dosage of his daily medications in a way that led to him being hospitalised. Then with his family able to say all their goodbyes, he expired peacefully. He succeeded in being able to give himself a dignified ending. *(Paragraphs 1 and 3 as related by her son Martin in Los Angeles.)*

On a day visit to Blackpool sitting by the side of a pool on which small yachts were plying in a gentle breeze our attention was caught by one of these whose two occupants obviously did not know how to manage a sailing-boat. Presently, as expected, it capsized and its occupants were thrown into the water. They started screaming and thrashing about when a man next to us shouted to them: 'stand up', which they did when the water only reached to their waist.

We were having dinner at a time when Jonathan was about 5 years old. He must have enjoyed the meal very much for at the end he ceremoniously got up and said: 'three cheers for the cook!' Fast forward about 30 years to when he and his family came to dinner, I took their younger son David to one side, told him the story and asked if he would do the same if he enjoyed the meal. At the appropriate time I prompted him and he rose to say: 'three cheers for the cooker'.

In this country we had always had a domestic animal of one kind or another. What was possibly unique with a black and white collie called Duke, a long-haired cat Fluffy and her son Sonny was that Duke helped Fluffy deliver her first and only litter of which we kept a ginger one Sonny. All three were great friends. Even more unique was that Duke and Sonny slept in the same basket cuddling up to one another.

An old lady gets a 'notice to pay' a bill of £500 which she did not have. She writes a letter to G"d asking for those £500 and addresses it to Him in Heaven. At the Post Office sorting office a postman at first holds the envelope up in ridicule, but eventually, having opened it, all the postmen have a 'whip-round' and collect the astonishing sum of £300. When the old lady receives this she writes another letter to G"d, thus: Dear G"d, I had asked for £500 but you only sent me £300. Where is the missing £200? Well, I suspect those people at the Post office".

Foreigners sometimes have difficulty pronouncing the 'th' in the English language. An ex-German coastguard was on duty when he heard a ship signalling on the radio 'we are sinking, we are sinking'. He radioed back 'what are you sinking about?'

In the 19c a young man called Dunkowski emigrated from his Polish village to England. His distraught mother made him promise to write giving his new address. He wrote that he lived in London WC 1, omitting the street name as in his village the postman knew everybody and where they lived; and that he had changed his name to Dunn. The mother wrote to the only address she had but of course the letter did not reach him. He therefor did not write back. Communication was lost. A year later another young man also emigrated to London. The mother of the first one asked him to locate her son and tell him off for not writing to his mother. When he got to London he went to the centre as a good starting point which was Piccadilly Circus. There he found to his delight WC, went downstairs where he found 1 [i.e. cubicle No.1] whose door was locked. He knocked on the door and shouted 'are you Dunn?' A voice from inside shouted 'yes'. From outside Dunn shouted back 'you swine, why don't you write to your mother?'

At a theatre performance of an adaptation of Anne Frank's 'Diary' the 'Germans' are going from room to room searching for Jews when a voice declaims from the audience – 'she's in the attic'.

A Palestinian boy wanted to blow himself and a building up with a suicide belt but he made a bad job of it and succeeded only in injuring himself becoming unconscious. The Israelis, true to their ethos of helping all whether enemy or friend, took him to hospital where, under an anaesthetic they repaired him. As he was slowly coming round he saw some good-looking nurses dancing round him and thought that he had arrived in Paradise as his elders had told him that he would meet 77 virgins there when he died.

A recruit for the Army was asked what languages he spoke. He said 'sanskrit'. When the officer asked him where they spoke that language the recruit said that it was the language of the Pharaos, so they sent him to the Faroe Islands.

An astronomer was giving a lecture and said, inter alia, that the sun would disappear in 6 billion years taking with it our civilisation. He invited questions and a man asked if he had said 6 million or 6 billion. The astronomer said that he had said 6 billion, whereupon the questioner said that he was relieved: for a moment, he thought that he had said 6 million.

Moses had led the Children of Israel through the desert for 40 years. At the end of the 39th year Mrs. Moses says to him: 'Is it not time you asked for directions?' (as related by Daniel Taub, one time Israeli Ambassador to the UK).

The cave in which Jesus was buried actually belonged to a man called Jonathan. When Jesus was buried there friends of Jonathan remonstrated with him that he had allowed a man who was not family to be buried in his cave. Jonathan replied that he was a good friend of his but, in any case, he would only be there for a long week-end (as related on BBC Radio 4 'Thought for the Day' by a bishop).

An American warship wanted to pay a courtesy visit to Vancouver, Canada but had to wait for a neap tide before it could enter the harbour because one of its masts was too high and would not pass under the bridge. It was then trapped waiting for the next neap tide before it could leave again.

At a formal dinner Winston Churchhill saw another guest put a silver ashtray into his pocket as guests were leaving. Quickly Churchhill also pocketed an ashtray, sidled up to the thief and taking out his ashtray and putting it on the table said to him: 'I think we have both been observed. We had better put them back where they belong' when the other guest had no choice but to follow suite.

I was fairly newly married to Marianne when we attended a party including Joan C. aged 6 who had a crush on me. We played a party game 'who would you like to be if you were not who you are?' Joan said 'Rudi' whereupon an adult guest Richard B. said she should have said Marianne.

On a cruise many years ago on the famous Cunard liner Queen Elizabeth 2 (QE 2) a huge electronic map was constructed in the atrium of the Atlantic Ocean with parts of land East and West and a line dawn across it to indicate the route the ship had taken with an X at the precise place where it was hour by hour. The X was just then by the Scilly Isles, marked in letters. One American lady said to her companion 'Look, we have just passed Sicily'.

A town in the North of England intended to purchase some obsolete London trams which had travelled along Kingsway. To ensure that they would fit the gauge, corners, bridges , etc. in the town a specimen was transported on a low loader and eventually found to be all right. The trams were bought and the first of them transported on the same low loader which, however got stuck under a bridge en route. On investigation they discovered that in between the first and the second consignment the road had been re-Macadamed and the level had been raised.

A visit to the USA coincided with the anniversary of the birth of Margaret Mitchell, author of 'Gone with the Wind.' To honour her the Post Office issued a 1c (!) stamp with her head and name. I bought a few for, by chance, a patient of mine was called by those names and the next time she attended I gave her one., much to her joy and amazement.

The director of the film 'Ben Hur' told his cameramen that as the chariot race was so difficult to mount he would only run it once as the substantive race without any rehearsal. After it was in the can he went from one cameraman to the next; he climbed the ladder on one such saying; 'did you get it?' when the man shouted down: 'ready when you are.'

A teacher wrote on a pupil's report that if … does not bring his homework into class he should not bother to come in, since when he had not seen him. (*The Times*)

A few years ago Anne Robinson had a TV show called 'The Weakest Link' in which she would ask questions of 15 contestants. She had a tendency to take every opportunity to be rude to these. One was a Welshman and she was rude about him and Wales which did not go down well in Wales, but it hit the headlines worldwide. She was invited by an American TV station to host a similar programme in the USA. Inevitably she herself was interviewed on chat shows. At this time 'The Times' newspaper ran a competition in which they would publish a photograph or cartoon inviting readers to compose a caption for it. One cartoon showed an interviewer asking Anne in a speech bubble: 'And where exactly in England is Wales?'

During World War Two two American soldiers were listening to a speaker at Marble Arch London, a famous site where anybody can stand, usually on a wooden box, and use the freedom of speech mantra to do just that, including, in the case of one man, criticising the conduct of the war, including making rude remarks about the King, Winston Churchhill, the Police, the Armed Forces, etc. A policeman sauntered over to the soldiers. They thought he would ask them to help him arrest the speaker, but he said: 'Switch off your [jeep's] engine – the poor chap cannot be heard.'

Steve Wonder, the American Jewish black and blind singer was once asked if being Jewish had been a detriment to his career. He replied that he did not think so but 'that it could have been worse – I could have been black.' (This story is partially fake)

In 2019 I gave a talk to a group of deaf people in the Synagogue about some aspects of Judaism. Three happenings attracted my attention. The first was that there was a tangible and friendly reaction when I put my own hearing aids in place in full view of the audience; the second was that they did not look at me as the speaker but to the signer standing a couple of meters away from me; the third was when I gave a blast on the shofar. A shofar is a ram's horn without a mouthpiece which is blown on the New Year

Festival and gives a note rather like a trumpet and as loud. They all heard that and reacted visibly. [When a friend read this she misread signer for singer and wondered why there should be a singer at a meeting of deaf people]. (The friend was Suzie Cree.)

A few decades after the Second World War German towns invited erstwhile citizens, who had to flee for religious or other reasons, back for a week, all expenses paid. Marianne and I spent a week in Berlin and at the end of the stay we were all invited to inspect the partially finished new Reichstag building. At the de-briefing afterwards the guide invited questions or comments. One of our group said: 'when I was in the top class of my school here in the 1930's I was asked to give a short dissertation in front of the class. When I had finished the teacher said that I had done this so well that, he thought, one day I would speak in the Reichstag. That prophesy has just been fulfilled'.

Marianne and I were in Israel after the 1967 war. The Golan Heights had been captured because they were used to shoot the occasional missile into Israel in the valley below. The guide told us not to cross white tapes which lined the sides of the path as there were still mines on the other side. One young boy walked perilously close to them and the guide admonished him saying the mines were very expensive to replace. One young Israeli woman who lived in the valley below the Heights and who joined the tourist excursion to see the view from where the Syrian soldiers had fired, went into hysterics not because of the perceived danger but because she realised that the soldiers might well have seen her sunbathing in the nude in her garden.

In a subsequent war a tank battle ensued in the Suez desert. At one point they churned up so much sand that the tanks from both sides tended to get mixed up and it became impossible to tell which were Israeli and which Egyptian. The Israeli tank commander told all Israeli drivers by radio to turn right on a given signal. Any tanks which did not turn right were enemy and automatically would become targets.

On a visit to Berlin, Germany, I passed a street market on the Ku'damm where a stall advertised the 'Koran' with a sign 'Liess den Koran'. My initial reaction was to interpret the first word as the English for 'lies', i.e. untruths. Only after a few seconds did I realise that it exhorted people to read it – liess = the imperative of the word lesen, to read.

My good fiend Zulfi Karim, the current President of the Bradford Council of Mosques, opened a restaurant a few years ago. At my fist visit and knowing that setting up a new venture is associated with high costs I deliberately ordered a sumptuous meal. When I came to pay he said as it was my first visit the meal would be 'on the house'.

A couple were looking at the Wagner Schauspielhaus (festival house) in Bayreuth, Germany when they became separated. The man took the opportunity to ask another tourist what this building was all about – he had no idea. After it was explained to him he shouted to his companion 'Brünnhilde, come here a minute'. [Brünnhilde is the principal female singer in Wagner's 'The Ring.']

I attended the 70th birthday party of Klaus Bandow, the third and only surviving son of my parents' best friends in Berlin. He was spokesman for BMW in Munich, Germany and he now had to retire. One of the guests said in his speech that 'at last he can drive a Mercedes car!'

Having been advjsed that drinking a half tumbler of warm mulled wine last thing at night would promote getting to sleep easily and have a good night's rest. I followed the advice and found that both were correct. One

207

morning, having benefitted from the advice, I went to the microwave and found the previous night's tumbler still there, undrunk. It must have exerted its influence by remote control.

Two teenagers kissed passionately but found on release that their respective orthodontic braces had got entangled. Another time a group of students crowded round a young patient who wore a complicated set of braces to which one of us said that with one wire more he would be able to hear America (by radio). Another student quipped 'not with one wire more but with one wire less.'

Having learnt Greek at school stood me in good stead when we were in Moscow, Russia and travelled on the Underground. I noticed a station name in cyrillic lettering and realised that we were going in the wrong direction.

Orchestral players know the music for 'Messiah' by Handel so well that they sometimes don't bother to look at the conductor. After a dress rehearsal the conductor was taken ill and the leader of the orchestra was asked to conduct the performance leaving an empty chair next to the deputy leader. At the next rehearsal the deputy leader asked the leader 'where were you last night?'

Booked into hotels in Buenos Aires, Hamburg and Moscow over the years we found two hotels of the same name in each of those towns. Having ordered a taxi to take us to the airport in one of these the taxi went to the wrong one which nearly caused us to miss our flight.

My late friend Rolf B. manufactured colloidal graphite which is a lubricant for heavy machinery. He voyaged from Hull to Rotterdam on a North Sea Ferry occupying an outside cabin. When he looked out of the window the next morning he found that the boat was still in Hull. When he asked a steward why? he said that there was some trouble with the engine; they had tried to telephone the company which supplied the lubricant for advice but there was no reply.

I got stuck in a lift twice in quick succession, once in a church in Leeds then again in a gurdwara (Sikh temple) in Bradford. Soon afterwards 'The Times' newspaper wrote something relevant to these occurrences so I wrote to say what happened to me. Patrick Kidd, journalist of the humorous column, wrote saying he must be careful not to get into a lift with me. I replied that, on the contrary, to get stuck is a rare misfortune, to get stuck a second time a great rarity, but the odds of getting stuck a third time must be astronomical and he would be quite safe.

A Jewish story: at the beginning of Passover families celebrate seder: festivities in the home as opposed to prayers in the synagogue. One of the rituals is to hide half a matzo (unleavened bread like a Jacobs cracker) for retrieval afterwards. My niece had constructed a zoom for family members in the pandemic but I had constructed in addition a seder table and as per tradition, hid the matzo, but so well that when it came to finding it I had forgotten where I had hidden it. Another ritual at seder is to drink four cups of wine at prescribed parts of the seder which I did, but not necessarily in the right order.

Moses had received the Ten Commandments hewn on to stone tablets on Mt. Sinai and now descended when he was faced with the Children of Israel worshipping a golden calf as if it were a god. In a fit of understandable anger he smashed the newly fashioned tablets on the ground. This was the first time that all Ten Commandments were broken at the same time.

Two families who were good friends lived in the Sudetenland of Czechoslovakia. When the Russians introduced communism in the country one family (G) escaped to Kaufbeuren, the other (H) to Niederoderwitz, both in Germany. When the DDR was formed H found themselves in communist country. Whilst G often crossed the border to visit their friends H bringing goods and food unobtainable in the DDR H could not leave the DDR except under the strictest rules which included that only one of a couple of working age could leave at a time (to prevent escape) and would be advised only one day before travel. Came an invitation to the wedding of the son of G for both H to come. They made an application to go knowing full well that it would be turned down. On the statutory one day before travel to their pleasant surprise they both got exit visas. The reason for the police chief's 'generosity' was that the wife of H was the manager of the care home in which the police chief's mother was a resident.

A man was understandably annoyed by molehills on his beautiful lawn. He advertised for someone to rid his lawn of moles. A man offered to do this and was asked to kill the moles the cruellest way possible because they had annoyed him so much. When the man had finished he was asked how he had killed the moles. The man said that he had buried them alive.

In summer a few years ago I wanted to buy some braces at George in Asda when I was told that they only sold them at Xmas time. [This is absolutely true].

When the start of Elon Musk's spaceflight in May 2020 was delayed by inclement weather one old lady thought it was because they were waiting for a full moon so as to present a larger target to aim for.

I was invited to recite (sing) the Jewish mourning song *el male rachamim* at the national annual Holocaust Memorial Event in Coventry, UK, a few years ago at the invitation of

Stephen Smith, founder of Beth Shalom, the Holocaust Memorial Centre in Laxton, Nottinghamshire. Afterwards at the reception Stephen came along with a smart looking lady on his arm and when he saw me stopped to introduce me to her. When I enquired who she was I was told that she was Hazel Blears MP, a well-known personality but whom I had never seen before, was suitably embarrassed and to make good gave her a tight embrace which she did not reject. Marianne who had been standing a little distance away saw this and now came forward asking 'what was going on here?' I explained who the lady was when Marianne said: 'well, that's all right, then.'

Two Dutch men and two Belgians were in the same railway compartment. The Dutch told the Belgians they would travel on only one ticket. Before the inspector came round they both went to the toilet. When the inspector knocked on the door they pushed just one ticket, their only one, under the door to be checked. The four met again another time when the Belgians said they would show the others that they would do the same but the Dutch said they would show them how to travel even without a ticket. The Belgians went to the toilet and one of the Dutch knocked on the door requesting tickets....

In the Council of Europe when a Member wishes to speak he/she is introduced by an interpreter who gives the name and district of the intending speaker. One such represented the French province of Normandy and was promptly introduced as M. ...who will give his Norman wisdom.

Some childrens' sayings: the French national anthem is La Mayonnaise. King Solomon had 300 wives and 700 porcupines. The Royal Mint is what the Queen pours over her roast lamb.

A surgery is where people insult their doctor. A father

gives his son a magnifying glass and advises him to use it only when there was something important to see.

He who laughs last, laughs best.

Addendum 3

Too late to be included in the text came the announcement on 17 October 2020 that I had been elected to the Hall of Fame for Bradford. To place it in context: previous Bradfordians who have been elected to this honour have included Barbara Castle, Timothy West, Sir Ken Morrison, Sir Tom Moore, J.B. Priestly and David Hockney.

On 12 November my MP Naz Shah mentioned me by name at the end of her speech about refugees in the House of Commons. Google Hansard, Search Hansard, Latest Sitting, 12 November 2020, Backbench Sitting, Right Arrow, Naz Shah at 2.30 p.m.

Addendum 4

George Bernard Shaw wrote a preface to some of his plays which were quite lengthy, robust and important. In that spirit I append a résumé of my family's achievements in age and generation order.

Children: Anthony was a manager for a firm which manufactured bone joints for humans, now retired; Judi was HR director for the holiday village Center Parcs, now retired; Jane was a travel agent for TUI, now retired; Jonathan is chief purser for the cruise line 'Cunard'; Lucy was a HL teaching assistant in a primary school, now retired; Deborah and Ged work for Bradford Metropolitan Council; Caroline works in quality assurance for a veterinary pharmaceutical company; Rob is account manager for a chemical testing laboratory.

Grandchildren: Louis is a self-employed stone mason; James is HART paramedic in Plymouth; Rebecca, having completed two years art course at one of the Liverpool universities, then having born Isabelle, is now studying child care; Matty, Rebecca's partner, is a delivery driver for Sainsbury's; David has a level-3 extended diploma in IT digital development with triple distinction currently selling telephones at Tesco awaiting an IT job; Daniel is a qualified motor mechanic and working as such; Eloise is a secretary; Alex, having completed a year at university studying dog training, is now employed by Boots the chemist as pharmacy adviser; Sophie and Oliver attend grammar school very successfully.

Great-grandchildren: Isabelle (2017) and Arlo (2020) are Wunderkinder.

I am justifiably extremely proud of my family, all high achievers, and so would Marianne's and my parents have been had they lived.

It might seem strange to have a Christian vicar write something for a faithful Jew, but for those of you who know Rudi, it won't come as a great surprise. Rudi has a wide and generous heart, committed to human flourishing in many different forms, breaking down misunderstanding and division, and seeking unity and harmony for the whole of humanity. Rudi is a faithful and practicing Jew who not only leaves his mark on the Bradford Synagogue, but on all the faith communities of West Yorkshire, where he lived and served the wider community. His singing on Remembrance Sunday and Holocaust Memorial Day for many years lives on in our hearts and minds – reminding us of Rudi and the story of Judaism, and of St Augustine, who says that He who sings prays twice! Rudi's story is one to be shared and celebrated.

The Revd Canon Hilary Barber, Halifax Minster

This is an important memoir. The detail and colour expose an experience that will too easily be forgotten in a new generation. Rudi's story keeps alive the memory of courage, community and faith when the worst evils of our world come to visit. A wonderful man has written an essential memoir.

The Rt Revd Nicholas Baines, Bishop of Leeds

I am honoured to write these few words. I have known Rudi for some 46 years and am pleased he has now published his family memoirs. He is an elder in age and wisdom but youthful in his manifold activities including his love for Bradford Synagogue, his musical talent, his Inter-Faith work, and his regular lectures in his birth country, Germany. Just one word describes Rudi, amazing!

Rabbi Douglas Charing, Director Jewish Education Bureau, and
Visiting Rabbi to Bradford Synagogue

I have had the utmost pleasure of Rudi's acquaintance on several occasions over the last ten years. He has worked inordinately hard for the Synagogue at Bradford and has always strived to promote inter-community faith. He has worked closely with the Sikh Community and myself as Chairman of the Yorkshire Sikh Forum. In recognition for his support and hard work we presented him with a Crystal trophy on the auspicious occasion of Visakhi.

Nirmal Singh MBE, FRSA, Uob

Reading Rudi Leavor's book Berlin to Bradford was a fascinating and inspirational read. I have seen the commitment he has made to good causes, not least that of his interfaith work. His early years experiences of the horrors of the Nazi regime did not create in him a 'victim' mentality. Instead he put every effort into being a positive human being working for the good of others. An exceptional role model for young people.

Baroness Margaret Eaton, OBE, DL

The city of Bradford will always be grateful that when Rudi Leavor and his family arrived as refugees from Nazi Germany, a clerk randomly sent them to Bradford. Rudi's extraordinary story now shines brightly in the story of this city, honest about the darkness of antisemitism and hatred, but also pointing to a better way in working with our different faith communities as we have learned to embrace one another.

The Very Revd Bishop Toby Howarth (of Bradford)

My association with redoubtable Rudi Leavor goes back over 35 years in many different ways but the most important part of our friendship and bonding has been the fact that we are both refugees: he from Nazi Germany and I from Uganda fleeing because of ethnic cleansing of Asians by Idi Amin in 1972.

Since my arrival in Bradford in 1981, I became acquainted and became friends with many Jewish people including Rudi and I was immediately impressed with his warm and friendly smiling face. Since then, I have worked with Rudi to promote Interfaith Harmony, Holocaust Memorial Services, Civic Events, Chanukah Celebrations and Educational visits at The Bradford Synagogue.

Rudi is an Old Boy of Bradford Grammar School and so are my son Dr Heman Joshi and daughter Megha Joshi which further cemented our friendship.

Rudi's outstanding and distinguished service given so freely and generously for Community Cohesion and Religious Harmony is a huge inspiration and ideal role model for everyone to emulate.

Rudi is a dentist by profession, is multi-talented, a gifted musician, singer and his ubiquitous presence at every event in Bradford & District has made him an icon of Bradford.

I'm delighted to be part of his life and this book which is a great account of a long, happy and fulfilling life dedicated in the service of Judaism and Humanity. Mazel Tov.

Dr Manoj N L Joshi DL, Hindu Faith

(Repeated) It's an honour to contribute a foreword to this memoir. This is an account of a life well and truly lived; a life dedicated to the service of others and to the bringing of understanding, peace and wellbeing between peoples. Rudi Leavor is a remarkable individual. In the following pages you will follow his remarkable journey, growing up as a Jewish child in Germany as the Nazis came to power, his family's flight to the UK and 'accidental' arrival in Bradford, his many years of service to the communities of Bradford and wider service to the Jewish community in the UK and beyond. At a time when our world seems ever more polarised and seismic tremors threaten to fracture relationships between communities Rudi's story remains as contemporary and important as ever. It is a privilege as Chief Executive of Bradford Council that I've been able to play a small part in bringing this project to fruition.

Kersten England CBE, Chief Executive, City Hall, Bradford

The publication of Rudi Leavor's memoirs sheds another ray of light on one of our world's darkest moments. For such a long time after the Holocaust the survivors felt unable to tell their personal stories but with the establishing of International Holocaust Memorial Day in the UK in 2001 many of us have been moved listening to many personal stories. For most scholars of the history of the Holocaust, survivor memoirs are regarded as an important reservoir of information and a crucial wellspring for filling gaps in our knowledge. I have known Rudi for the past twenty years and reading his memoirs has helped me to fill in many gaps in my knowledge.

Bishop Tony Robinson, Bishop of Wakefield

I am proud to have known Rudi Leavor for many years. He has played a significant role in the interfaith network of Bradford and is highly respected for the work he does. He brings together people of all faiths and none, with a gentle spirit and wise words. He is an important part of the faith fabric of Bradford and we are richer for his example. I have huge respect for his contribution and deep faith, anyone who has heard him sing in the synagogue cannot fail to be moved.

Imran Hussain, MP

I thoroughly enjoyed reading my good friend Rudi's story. A comprehensive overview of his life, from details about Rudi's childhood and family, the arrest of his parents, the tragedy of losing close family members in Auschwitz to arriving in Bradford and so much more. Personally, for me Rudi is a shining star, who not only guides me but is also an inspiration and credit to the people of Bradford and beyond. I am extremely proud of all Rudi's achievements and this book is a must read for everyone.

Naz Shah, MP

Rudi's life is a story of suffering and joy through great challenge and opportunity. To meet Rudi in person is to encounter a person of profound openness and a deep generosity of spirit and those qualities shine through the tone and detail of these memoirs.

The Reverend Canon Sam Corley, Rector of Leeds

BV - #0036 - 031220 - C33 - 229/152/11 - PB - 9781914002021